Robert Grant

The Knave of Hearts

A Fairy Story

Robert Grant

The Knave of Hearts
A Fairy Story

ISBN/EAN: 9783744665315

Printed in Europe, USA, Canada, Australia, Japan

Cover: Foto ©Thomas Meinert / pixelio.de

More available books at **www.hansebooks.com**

THE

KNAVE OF HEARTS

A Fairy Story

BY

ROBERT GRANT

AUTHOR OF

"THE CONFESSIONS OF A FRIVOLOUS GIRL," "AN AVERAGE MAN,"
"THE LITTLE TIN GODS-ON-WHEELS," ETC.

BOSTON AND NEW YORK
HOUGHTON, MIFFLIN AND COMPANY
The Riverside Press, Cambridge
1894

The Riverside Press, Cambridge, Mass., U. S. A.
Electrotyped and Printed by H. O. Houghton & Company.

"*Vixi puellis nuper idoneus*
   Et militavi non sine gloria."

"*Nunc arma defunctumque bello*
   Barbiton hic paries habebit."

I.

"HE shall be a lawyer and go to Congress," said my father.

"He shall be a banker and control railroads," said my mother.

These were very natural assertions, for I was the descendant of distinguished families on both sides. My maternal great-grandfather was killed at Bunker Hill, my maternal grandfather was a judge of the Supreme Court of the United States, while my father's folk for several generations had been merchant princes.

I was an only son, and my three sisters, sitting side by side on the sofa, with luxuriant fluffy golden hair flowing over their shoulders, looked very proud at the parental prophecies. Yet, like true daughters of a free soil, they were not content to have their opinions formed for them. Cried Alice Maud, the eldest, a maiden of fifteen summers: —

"O mamma, I do hope Arthur will be a sailor! I adore sailors!" She knocked the heels of her little bronzed kid boots together in her ecstasy.

"No, dear Alice," said Julia Pierson, who was quiet and pensive, yet a firm child; "he would look much nicer in canonicals. I should love to see him a clergyman."

Medora (my mother had pleased herself in the choice of a name for the youngest) shook her yellow mane like a colt in her impatience at the choice of her sisters.

"How hateful, Julia! And I don't care much for sailors, either! They walk all crooked." The child slightly protruded her nine-year-old tongue. "I want him to be an actor and go on the stage."

I, the subject of this dialogue, sat meanwhile with one leg thrown listlessly over the arm of a chair smoking a cigarette. I was just graduated from college, and very well content with my own importance. Something was to become of me in the future, I knew, but the precise character of my destiny I was disposed to leave to the selection of others. It was sufficient for me now to be aware that the points of my collar met unexceptionably, and that my mustache was waxing in importance daily. Nevertheless, I fingered the ends of the latter between the puffs, and assumed a slightly meditative air. After all, my affairs were being discussed, and mere politeness demanded some display of interest on my part.

A short pause followed the infant Medora's expression of opinion. It seemed almost as if the family were awaiting a remark from still another source. The delay was not long, however, for a frail cough from an obscure corner of the room was followed by an old woman's quaver : —

"You are all of you wrong, my dears; he is to be the Knave of Hearts."

To say that my family regarded my great-great-aunt as a witch would be to ascribe to them a degree of superstition incompatible with the times in which we live. I dare say some of my ancestors would not have hesitated long to hurry the old gentlewoman to the stake, but, thank Heaven! no one has faith in witchcraft to-day; and when my mother wished to account for Aunt Selina's idiosyncrasies, she was wont simply to speak of her as "peculiar." Everybody was quite satisfied with that explanation.

"What nonsense!" said my mother.

"What do you mean by that?" asked my father.

"How interesting!" cried Alice Maud.

"How volatile!" observed Julia Pierson, who had a command of language.

"Then he won't go on the stage," whimpered little Medora.

As for me, I continued to twirl my mustache thoughtfully, with my eyes fixed on my patent-leather shoes, which were quite new and objects of pride.

"Mark my words, he will be the Knave of
Hearts," repeated the aged dame; whereupon
she hobbled out of the room, letting fall in passing the ball of worsted attached to her knitting,
which rolled away and fastened itself around
one of the legs of the piano.

I think my family must have looked upon
her words in the light of an anathema, for they
gazed at each other almost ruefully. But I, who
have never shared the awe of the old lady felt
by the rest of the household, proceeded to pick
up her property and follow the trail of the yarn,
which continued to unwind itself in keeping
with Aunt Selina's steps. It was a genuine
labyrinth I was pursuing, for my venerable relative lived in a wing of the house which was quite
uninhabited save for her occupancy. She was
my father's great-aunt on his mother's side, and
had lived with us ever since I could remember.
Long experience had taught the family to give
her sayings consideration, for there was apt to
be much more pith therein than appeared at
first sight. It was customary with us all to ask

Aunt Selina's advice before taking any important step, and though, as in the present case, her utterings would sometimes excite apparent incredulity, they were sure to sink deep into the hearts of the hearers.

When the ball of worsted had regained its former proportions, I found myself at the door of her apartment, which was still open.

"Look, aunt," said I, advancing; "you dropped this in the sitting-room, and I have brought it to you."

She received the ball from me with a gracious nod of the head, and was probably prepared for my immediate departure. But with a self-composure, which was a trait of mine that never deserted me, I slipped into an easy-chair and resumed the stroking of my mustache and the survey of my boots. The old lady had established herself already in her favorite straight-backed seat, and the click of her knitting-needles was the only sound audible in the room. Once I stealthily raised my eyes and caught sight of a smile hovering upon the withered lips. It was

plain to me that she was not vexed at my presence. I determined, however, to await develop-
ments, for I was a diplomat by nature.

Presently she arose, and, going to a cup-
board, took therefrom a bottle upon which dust
still lingered, and two glasses.

"That is Madeira, Arthur, bottled half a
century before you were born."

I bowed gravely, and, raising to my lips the
glass which she presented me, tasted the precious
fluid with an air of respect, yet nevertheless
critically. Often as I had visited her apartments,
my aunt never before had offered me wine.

"It is very old," I observed, holding the
golden liquor to the sunlight. "What is its
precise age, aunt?"

"I cannot say to a certainty. The wine was
given me by Captain Michael Westering just
before he sailed upon his last voyage, in the
year 1813. It had been in his possession more
than a decade."

I listened with reverence, yet with curiosity,
for from the sigh which escaped her I came to

the conclusion that this Captain Westering must have been the hero of a romance familiar to me since childhood. It was a family secret that Aunt Selina in youth had been loved by and reciprocated the attachment of a famous mariner, a mysterious personage whose methods upon the deep were not wholly free from suspicion. Indeed, his reform was, I believe, made a condition of their marriage; but the bridegroom disappeared upon the eve of the wedding, having been lost at sea, according to popular report, while returning from a voyage to the coast of Guinea. Despite many flattering offers, Aunt Selina had remained true to his memory through all these years. The captain had neglected to make a will in her favor, but this circumstance did not a whit impair her constancy. *Those who love well love but once*, was the moral which the narrators of her story loved to dwell upon.

I had never heard the name of her lover mentioned. My mother, whose knowledge of the affair was my own source of information,

THE KNAVE OF HEARTS.

always spoke of him as "the Captain," and
I do not believe that my father, whose relative she was, knew more than this. To have
questioned Aunt Selina upon the subject would
have exceeded the audacity even of my sister,
Julia Pierson, whom a desire for truth rendered
callous to the ordinary canons of taste.

My aunt sipped a glass of wine and wiped
her lips with a handkerchief, the exquisite lace
embroidery of which was yellow with time.
She had a thin face, with a peaked chin and
small ferret eyes. Her nose was a marked
aquiline. She wore no cap, and her hair,
which, though snow-white, was still abundant,
lay smooth as wax upon either side of the part,
and culminated at each temple in a knob-like
bunch of curls. Her dress was precise in its
neatness, but of extreme simplicity. A straight
gown of black silk, unrelieved by ornament
or conventionalized by crinoline, had been her
costume as far back as my memory extended.

"You have become a man, Arthur," she
said at length, as if by way of preface.

I inclined my head with dignity, and pinched my upper lip expectantly.

"I am an old woman now. Folk call me an old maid, I daresay."

"You should not talk so, aunt." The maiden lady had passed her eighty-second birthday, but I never was deficient in tact. "Indeed," said I, with a boldness that was surprising to myself, "does not the world know that a single life is of your own choosing?"

She looked up at me and chuckled exultantly. "Ay, ay," she squeaked, "I was not mistaken, I was not mistaken."

"Mistaken in what, aunt?"

"In you, my dear. You are to be the Knave of Hearts." She rubbed together her bony hands, and for some minutes mumbled inaudibly in her delight.

"I, too, was young once, but I was a fool," she said. "You will be wiser."

"You talk in riddles, aunt; please explain;" and leaning forward, I bent my deep brown eyes upon her caressingly, for I was said to possess winning ways.

"I gave him my whole heart, forever and forever. He carried it away with him, and I never saw him again," cried the old woman, with a voice that was between a sigh and a hiss. "It was a mistake."

"Did he not give you his in return, Aunt Selina?" I queried.

"Fiddlesticks!" was the reply.

I realized that my question had disappointed my relative's estimate of my intelligence. Even in asking it I had been conscious that it was weak and boyish.

"You will never be so foolish," she continued, emphatically.

Here was an opportunity to retrieve my lost ground: "I trust not, I am sure, aunt."

"I was just eighteen," she went on to say. "I was young, and had no one to advise me. Besides, he was very handsome."

There was a slight touch of vanity in the tone of her last words, which neutralized the self-reproach of what went before, and fumbling in her pocket she drew forth a leather case containing a miniature which she held out for my inspection. I turned it to the light and gazed upon the features of a dashing youth of commanding presence, whose hair was of the shade of a raven's wing, and whose eyes seemed still instinct with life, so radiant were they with the lustre of a keen vitality. Involuntarily I uttered an expression of admiration.

"Yes," she continued, "he was indeed beautiful. That is the sole excuse which I have to offer for my folly. But how paltry does it seem when I reflect upon the desert of time that separates me from my eighteenth year; a period during which I might have known much and varied happiness, had I been less prodigal of my heart in early youth. A portion of it would have satisfied the captain, and I should not be to-day a spinster, whose hueless existence supplies food to chroniclers of musty romance. Imbecile that I was, I gave him the whole."

"It was an error, — an error of judgment undoubtedly," I answered. "You left yourself quite at the mercy of circumstance, as the event proved. Naturally, having given your whole heart, you could not marry again. Am I right in my conjecture?" While awaiting her response I ventured to help myself again to Captain Westering's Madeira.

It was some minutes before Aunt Selina resumed the conversation, and then her words indicated a step forward in the line of thought.

"You are the only one of the family, Arthur, upon whom I feel that I can rely for sympathy and appreciation. Your father sacrificed himself in his twentieth year to a sentiment that is more ardent and commonplace to-day than at its inception. Life lay before him, bright with opportunity, but he, like myself, fell a victim on the threshold to the infatuation of a single absorbing passion. Firm believer as I am in the laws of heredity, I have some confidence that you may be exempt from this ancestral curse."

I inclined my head in token of gratitude for her good opinion, and she proceeded with the subject.

"You are handsome, Arthur: more so even than your father at the same age. There was a certain robust rigor in his composition that is softened in yours."

"My only weak point, aunt, is my nose. It is somewhat large. But I am not one to become dejected over a trifle, and have every reason to be content with my personal appearance."

"And yet I have known young people as well endowed as you, my nephew, marry within six months after their majority. There was, I remember, a contemporary of mine, — a tall, magnificent creature, with an alabaster skin and the lips of a Hebe, — who threw herself away at seventeen during an ocean passage. It was sheer folly, for the man was of the persevering kind, and would have waited any number of years, — years which would have been everything to her."

"I have had some slight experience in such matters already," said I, with a conscious blush which annoyed me withal, but was very likely imperceptible to Aunt Selina, whose eyes were no longer what they used to be. "There was a girl"—

"Enough, Arthur," interrupted the old lady. "It is not my desire to pry into your private affairs. Have I not stated already that I have confidence in you ? If indeed your allusion relates to the friendship you enjoyed with a certain young person during your vacation last summer, let me add that I was no blind observer of your behavior; I may say she had every reason to imagine that you were desperately fond of her. Even I was almost deceived by your show of admiration, and trembled to think of the probable upshot of the affair; for I could not help remembering that you were your father's son and my grandnephew. The result has proved me to be mistaken, and has confirmed my previous estimate of your intelligence."

"And yet, aunt," I asked, with a contraction of my brow (for with all my due appreciation of my parts I was a modest man, and doubtful of the extent to which I should be justified in presuming upon my capacity), "do you mean that you advise me to regard my individuality in this respect as a calling?"

"Why not, my dear? Is there any other, pray, for which you are better fitted? There is many a young lawyer and doctor who would gladly exchange his profession for yours had he the qualifications which you possess."

"But," I faltered, "how am I to provide myself with means of support, for you are aware that my father, though in comfortable circumstances, is not so wealthy as to warrant me in continuing to be a burden upon him."

Aunt Selina made a gesture of impatience. "Do not concern yourself as to means. They will be found readily enough as the occasion requires. You have too much ability and good sense ever to come to want. Still, if the worst arrives, it will be always in your power to marry an heiress, though I deprecate such a proceeding for many years to come. There is one thing, however, that I advise: Have a nominal calling of some kind besides, — a lawyer's, a cotton-

broker's, or any other that is reputable, and yet
where you will be your own master. In this
community a young man who cannot lay his
finger on his occupation and say I am this, that,
or the other arouses suspicion."

She paused, quite exhausted by this long ex-
hortation, to which I listened with rapt attention
and a growing respect for her knowledge of
human nature.

In answer to my inquiry as to the advisability
of entering upon my vocation at once, Aunt
Selina counselled expedition.

"While the next few years will doubtless
add to your powers of fascination, the bloom
of early manhood has a potency of its own not
to be undervalued. Time may teach you the
art of employing your talents to greater ad-
vantage, but no amount of sophistication can
simulate the freshness of youth."

Therewith she laid aside the knitting with
which her hands were busied, and seeking an
antique mahogany escritoire which rested upon
brass supports in the guise of a griffin's claws,

produced a miniature horse-hair trunk. Its contents proved to be a packet of letters tied about
with a faded lavender ribbon, and an ivory box
of elaborate Eastern workmanship. Pressing a
spring in the latter she disclosed a curious
trinket, resembling in form, color, and size a
veritable human heart. At Aunt Selina's instance I took it from its receptacle, and found
that though the surface of the bauble was
smooth as ivory, it was plastic to the touch.
While I was wondering greatly regarding its
composition I heard my kinswoman say with
a sigh, —

"This heart was given me in the year 1813
by Captain Michael Westering, as a pledge of
unalienable and unqualified affection."

The tremor of her voice prompted me to look
up from my examination of the treasure, and
I observed that the eyes of my ancestress were
moist with tears. Upon perceiving that I was
aware of her mood, she dashed the drops away
with a movement of her ancient knuckles, and
emptying upon the table the remaining content

of the little box, drew from a heap of rubbish that might once have been a nosegay a lancet in the form of an arrow. Its point was the blade, and the shaft, which was of raised silver, terminated in a minikin of a cupid after the manner of an apostle spoon.

"What is that, my aunt?" I asked, with a view to help her to regain her composure by a delicate ignoring of her emotion.

She passed the lace handkerchief across her lips once or twice, and took another sip of wine before replying.

"That is a keepsake given to me by the family of Captain Westering after his fate had ceased to be questioned. It has rested all these years in the dusty embrace of the first and last posies he ever bestowed upon me. It is but natural, Arthur," she went on to say after a pause, "that the unearthing of these memorials of my youth should unnerve me for an instant. One cannot always, by the mere exercise of the will, master a despised weakness. You are scientist enough to understand that the muscles

often refuse to obey the behest of the intelligence. But enough of this. I have brought
forth these trinkets for a purpose. They are
for you to make use of, my nephew. This
heart is composed of material which, though of
extreme tenacity, cannot withstand the keen
blade of its companion. Take them both and
wear them in the pocket on the left side of your
waistcoat, which I see is still empty. The time
may come in the course of your experience
when they will prove of service. If it should
ever chance — as I believe it will — that you are
tempted to place your whole heart at the disposal of another, I counsel you to recall at that
instant my example and my precept. At such
a time forbear to give your whole heart; but
if it is your desire to leave a symbol with her
whose charms seem for the moment superlative,
slice off a portion of this token with the lancet
and replace the rest in your pocket. The satisfaction of the morrow will indemnify you a
hundred-fold for the transient pain of self-control. Heaven bless you, my nephew!"

So saying she placed the box in my hands, and I, with that gallantry which has ever been a part of my nature, stooped to touch my lips to the faded fingers. There was a fascination, doubtless, about my manner of so doing that appealed to the old lady, for she chuckled again with manifest satisfaction.

" I have no fear for you, my nephew."

" Nor have I for myself, in sooth, aunt, thanks to your counsel and vade-mecum."

" Rogue ! " she murmured, " were it not that the captain has my heart, verily I might be your first victim."

" Not the first, Aunt Selina," I said, perhaps less modest for the nonce than my wont; " you forget my summer's episode. But at least," I added, " you will not object to a piece of my heart, even if you prize it not ; " and, suiting the action to the words, I had sliced *off* a small section of the composition article before she could interpose an objection.

" Stay, foolish boy ! " she cried, though she was not displeased. " Waste not your treasure on an old spinster like me. You will need it all, I daresay." She took the heart from my hand, and proceeded to restore it to its original condition by dint of a little glue. " There ! " she exclaimed, in a delighted falsetto, " it looks as good as whole. No one ever would know that it had been scratched, unless she were to examine it very carefully. Once more, good-by, my dear; for I am weary after so unwonted an interview."

We were sitting at tea one evening about a week later when I surprised the family by the announcement that I was contemplating a short journey.

" For what reason? " asked my father, pausing in the demolition of a piece of buttered toast.

" I am going away on business," I responded gravely.

" But it was only yesterday that you put up · your sign as a lawyer."

I made no reply to this remark, for I felt sure my father would not sympathize with my real reason for departure, and I was no skilful hand at dissimulation. To tell the truth, Aunt Selina's suggestions had so worked upon my fancy that I was eager to test my ability elsewhere than at home. It was she who now came to my rescue.

" The boy needs some diversion after his four years of study. He ought not to settle down to work until he has seen a little of the world," piped the old lady in a friendly key. " Here, Arthur," she continued, reaching across to me a handful of gold coins of no small denomination, " these will enable you to prolong your journey and enjoy yourself for a few weeks after the completion of the business by which you are called away."

The sight of the money must have had a soothing effect upon my parent, since he did not remonstrate further against my going; nay, he even began presently to enlarge upon the advantages to be derived from travel, and counselled me to keep my eyes open while absent from my native city. He declared that the knowledge acquired and acquaintances made upon such an occasion might be of great use to me in my subsequent legal career.

"And when do you propose to start?" he inquired finally.

"To-morrow morning."

"Mercy!" cried my mother, and she hurried out of the room to give orders that such of my wardrobe as was in the wash should be put in proper condition.

My golden-haired sisters Alice and Medora clambered to my lap and nestled their heads on my shoulder.

"It must be too lovely for anything to travel. I wish I were going with you," said the eldest.

"Ah!" whispered little Medora, with a sigh of childish envy, "he will see real lions and live princesses. Do bring us home something awfully nice, Arthur, dear."

But Julia Pierson sat apart and looked unhappy. At last she said, in a tone of disappointment which was not without reproof, "I thought he was going to stay at home and marry Leila Johnson."

Now, Leila Johnson was the young lady to whom I had been attentive the preceding summer.

"My dears," cried Aunt Selina, in a tone of authority, from her obscure corner, "your brother is to be the Knave of Hearts."

II.

A passing glance at the occupants of the parlor-car in which I was to travel gave me a sense of disappointment. I scanned each individual in turn, but not once did my eye kindle with the lustre of awakened sympathy. My fellow-passengers were of an uninteresting class. My right-hand neighbor was an old lady who fidgeted as to the bestowal of her belongings, which included sundry carpet-bags, a geranium plant wrapped in newspapers, and a canary. Dire, to say the least, were my reflections as I surveyed the situation.

The chair directly opposite to me across the aisle was still vacant, and I had leisure to meditate that my well-being for the next few hours would depend largely upon the character of its

occupant. Let the new-comer be as uncon-
genial as the persons by whom I was surrounded, and a tedious day was in store for
me; but if, as it was only reasonable to expect,
the mediocre average of those present should
chance to be relieved by —

My deliberations were cut short by the sound
of voices at the entrance of the car. The porter, bearing wraps and a neat Russia-leather
bag, preceded a thin middle-aged lady and two
girls. One of these, though comely, had the
spare physique of her elder companion; but the
other was a laughing, rosy-faced young woman
of a decidedly stunning type. For an instant
I experienced a painful doubt as to which of the
trio was to be my fellow-traveller, but their conversation speedily put an end to my discomfort.

"My dear," said the elder lady, addressing
her of the glowing cheeks, "we shall miss you
dreadfully."

"I feel quite broken-hearted at the thought
of leaving you. I have had a perfectly heavenly
time," was the reply.

"I don't know what I shall do without you, Blanche," said the slim young lady.

"You must write to me, Emily, very often."

The porter had placed the bag, which I noticed was marked with the letters B. L., beside the vacant chair across the aisle; and as the ladies were grouped in very close quarters I delicately left my seat, with the hope that one of them would occupy it until the departure of the train. At this moment I observed Emily, under whose demure air a spice of mischief lurked, whisper something to her friend, who blushed and tittered slightly.

"What nonsense, Emily! He won't do anything of the kind."

"You just wait and see, dear."

The speaker pressed her face against the window-pane, as if she expected to catch a glimpse of some one outside. Blanche stood at her elbow, and tried, by giggling protestations, to interrupt this action, though I fancied she was far from displeased thereby.

I wandered out to the platform of the car

and lighted a cigarette. After a few pensive puffs I drew from my pocket a small note-book, the virgin page of which I inscribed as follows: —

No. 1. Blanche L——.
Residence, New York (probably).
Blonde; superb physique; fine animal spirits; giggles.

MEMORANDA.

Has been visiting in Boston and has received attentions. Expects admirer at depot. Will be dis-appointed if he does not bring flowers.
Verb. Sap.

Alighting from the car, I began to walk up and down with my hands behind my back. A few minutes must still elapse before the departure of the train. Just then I saw a win-dow open and Emily's delicate face peep out expectantly. I could almost feel the sympa-thetic squeeze of the hand she doubtless gave Blanche, who leaned upon her shoulder. They plainly were beginning to fear that the tardy admirer was not coming. But I was by no means of their opinion. I felt certain he would arrive. In all probability the florist had disappointed him, and he was ransacking the town for roses.

The gate through which passengers obtained admission to the train was in the rear of the last car, and practically out of range from the Pullman. I sauntered thither. A queue of people filed past me with movements of haste. It lacked but two minutes of the hour. I stepped beyond the wicket into the area of the depot. All was confusion. Passengers were scurrying hither and thither, for there were several other trains in process of arrival and departure. I looked searchingly among the crowd, but there was no sign of the missing youth.

A bell in the office struck warningly. I stood with my watch in hand. Blanche was right. He was not coming. And yet such deliberate desertion struck me as so inartistic as to render me incredulous even at this late moment.

As I replaced my watch in my fob I perceived a figure describing a rapid course through the crowd in the station. By the fashionable cut of his clothes and the green pasteboard box he carried, I recognized the tardy lover. I started toward him with some impetuosity and we came into collision.

"I beg your pardon, sir!" I exclaimed, with the courtesy at my command on all occasions.

The young man, who was almost breathless with hurry, looked as if he could have strangled me on the spot, but with the self-control of good breeding swallowed his wrath, and somewhat fiercely demanded which was the New York train.

"It is there," I cried, pointing to one at the opposite corner of the platform.

He sped like a deer in the direction indicated, and I just had time to pass through the wicket before it closed sharply. I ran forward and caught the railing of my car, which was already in motion. The buxom Blanche stood upon the platform waving her handkerchief to her two friends, who followed the advancing train with similar snowy signals of farewell. There was a rueful expression upon the face of Miss Emily, as if she harbored sympathy for the other's disappointment. The victim looked back smilingly, however.

" Be sure and write soon."

" Yes, dear; and I'm certain there's some mistake," cried Emily, throwing a kiss as a last greeting.

I took my seat, and for nearly an hour interested myself by looking out at the scenery. The fortunate course of events had swathed my soul in a sort of glamour, so that the houses and fields and hills and valleys flying past in swift succession served as a background for the play of my imagination. I found an exquisite pleasure in giving the rein to fancy, and indulging in that adulation of feminality frequent with me even when propinquity furnished no cause; for I had ever cherished an ideal in regard to the gentler sex. I had a limitless faith in woman, and yearned to encounter the spirit in whose companionship my every aspiration would find content.

Here she was perhaps close at hand. I stole a glance at my neighbor across the aisle, who was sitting twirling the fringe of her sack with a thoughtful air. The memory of her sibilant giggle haunted my ear as the rhythm of a cool mountain brook recalled in the passages of a fever. She was a splendid piece of flesh and blood, whom a pensive brow no more became than a dull sky the laughing stream. A wealth of curling tow-colored hair flowed from under the arch of her bonnet, and dimples nestled in the curves of her fresh-hued cheeks. Instinct told me that the life which even now bubbled upon the margin of those red lips would soon reassert itself and dissipate her disappointment. Take vitality and pique together, and you have the material for a runaway.

I was in the course of transferring this epigram to my note-book when the news-agent passed through the car with a collection of the literature of the day. I stealthily took note that the two novels he placed upon the lap of my fair companion bore severally the titles of " True to the Last" and "A Lass of Spirit." She examined the first of these with a pensive interest, but, though she sighed once or twice in the course of turning the pages, she ended by selecting the other.

There is an old adage in regard to the danger of letting a hot iron cool, which came to my mind at this juncture. I felt the necessity of bestirring myself instantly. The delicacy of my nature had prompted me to leave Blanche to her own reflections until now, but I must confess I began to fear that in my consideration for her feelings I might have prejudiced my own interests. Her recovery from her discomfiture had been more rapid than my estimate of feminine character gave me reason to expect. The wound not only had had time to smart, but to begin to heal.

An opportunity was not long lacking. The volume purchased proved to be one the pages of which were uncut, and as she was wavering between the alternative of employing her index finger and laying the book aside, I hastened to

offer her an ivory paper-cutter which belonged
to my travelling-bag. It was a plain but tasteful affair, with my monogram blazoned upon
the handle.

She expressed her thanks by a smiling, but
ladylike, inclination of the head; and I noticed,
as she made use of the instrument, a faint blush
suffuse her cheek, and creep upward to the
roots of her hair.

A quarter of an hour later I aided her to
raise a window which resisted her (as I decided) half-hearted pressure, and when the
train stopped ten minutes for refreshments,
asked her to permit me to get her something
to eat. Her refusal was expected, for I felt
morally certain that her reticule contained a
supply of sandwiches; but the opportunity was
not one to be neglected.

Nor was I mistaken, for when we emerged
from the dimness of the way-station she produced a packet of chicken and bread wrapped
in a snowy doily. I was not conscious of
hinting, by any expression of countenance, a

desire to share her repast, but perhaps it was
my having no luncheon of my own that led her
to ask timidly, if I would not take a sandwich.
After proper hesitation I accepted her offer,
and the opportune removal to the smoking-car
of a gentleman who occupied the chair next to
her's gave me a chance to establish myself at
her side and venture a few remarks.

Our conversation was necessarily very formal
for the first few minutes, but the discovery of
mutual friends in both New York and Boston
broke the ice and established a bond of sympathy between us.   The enthusiasm of her
manner completely charmed me, and she made
use of very extravagant adjectives to express
satisfaction regarding trivial matters.

I was altogether happy. She appeared to
me the most fascinating person I had ever met.
Her fresh beauty filled me with admiration,
for under the influence of excitement her eyes
seemed lakes of liquid blue. I tried my best
to be agreeable, and having come to the conclusion that she preferred to laugh, drew largely

on my stock of stories and witticisms. Whenever I essayed any topic of a more serious nature a sort of embarrassment clothed her strict attention, as if implying that my quasipedantry was alarming. In response to queries regarding her opinions on the Irish question and a recent publication, she responded, " Oh, yes," and became unnaturally grave. Clearly she would consider me very uninteresting were I to continue in this fashion.

So, when I had come to the end of the tales and conundrums at my command, I showed her one or two tricks with coins that could be performed without attracting too much attention in the car. She was sure she could imitate them, and her fruitless efforts at success kept us in continuous mirth. I propounded to her that venerable query the answer to which is "the little boy lied," and was amply rewarded for my pains, since it appealed extraordinarily to her risibility, though she declared with a shake of her shoulders, by way of feigned anger, that I was "awfully unkind" to make

sport of her. The innocent device of knotting
my handkerchief until it bore some resemblance to a rabbit, and causing it to jump spas-
modically in imitation of that creature, fairly
convulsed my lovely companion, and strength-
ened our friendship. The strictly impersonal,
however, does not long satisfy any woman. So
my natural instinct warned me, and I turned by
degrees the course of conversation into a more
interesting channel. A few direct and simple
questions were necessary for the acquirement
of one or two facts in regard to herself, but I
avoided abandoning more than momentarily the
jester's part. Anything in the nature of abstract discussion, which I knew to be an artistic
and convenient veil for sentiment, would, in the
case of Blanche, be out of place. Badinage
was the only available method of paying tribute
to her fascinations or interesting her in one's
own.

I found that compliments, when couched in
a not too serious tone of voice, pleased her
greatly. The more delicate ones were not so

effective as those easily understood. She pretended to think these laudatory speeches very ridiculous, and accused me of being foolish. Leaning slightly over the back of her chair, I would whisper some still more extravagant bit of flattery as a reply, to be greeted very likely with a declaration that she would have nothing more to do with me. By way of carrying out her threat she would look fixedly in the opposite direction.

"Miss Lombard," said I (I had discovered her name to be Blanche Lombard), "do you dot your eyes?"

My query concealed a society inanity I had heard exploded not long before.

Her head was turned the other way, and she seemed deaf to my utterance.

"At least you might answer a civil question," I continued.

There was no response. I thought I could detect a muffled giggle.

"You make a great mistake if you do, for they are *capital* eyes."

" How absurd !　What nonsense you do talk !"

She looked still more fixedly away from me, and twisted her shoulders so as to exclude all view of her face.

" But it is true, Miss Lombard.　I am only speaking the truth.　If you do not believe me, judge for yourself.　Here is the opportunity." So saying, I drew from my pocket one of those round, flat pin-cushions carried by men, the back of which contained a mirror.

She turned her head a little in her curiosity to see what this was, but immediately looked the other way again.　While in this position she put out her hand suddenly and took the pin-cushion from me.

" Philopena ! " I cried.

We had formed an agreement not five minutes before that whoever of us should first receive anything from the hand of the other should pay a forfeit.　In the event of my losing, her prize was to be five pounds of bonbons.　If I won, she was to make me a tobacco-pouch.

The moment I uttered the fatal word Blanche made an exclamation that would doubtless have been a little shriek had the surroundings permitted.

" Oh ! " she cried, with an indignant writhe of her whole figure, *"you horrid thing! I never will speak to you again."*

The excitement of her manner, which found a partial vent in the intensity of these expressions, caused me a thrill of sweet satisfaction. She seemed to me positively an angel, and I was conscious that the epithet, " you horrid thing," embodied the highest note in her gamut. The quintessence of enraptured vitality was condensed therein, and I was the fortunate being who had evoked it.

From this culmination of the climax the conversation gradually declined in interest, and I shortly had the tact to withdraw and leave my companion to her own meditations. I sought the smoking-car, and, lighting another cigarette, gave myself up to a reverie which would have been wholly delicious but for the lurking doubt as to my chances for success. I did not question that I had made an impression on my fellow-traveller; but would she regard me as other than a mere incident of the journey, a transient influence, which would cease to operate upon the morrow? Was she still free, or were there a score of lovers at her feet? What was the true footing upon which the swain stood whose flowers I had so lately anticipated? He might, for aught I could tell, be on the eve of conquest, and I the plaything of an hour. I loved — I realized the condition well — deeply and passionately, and all the tortures of a doubting spirit were mine. In the fulness of my infatuation I drew out my note-book once more and wrote as follows : —

" *You horrid thing! I never will speak to you again.*"

This shibboleth, still pregnant with the timbre of her voice, floated through the chambers of my brain.

As I completed the last word, I perceived that we had almost reached our destination. I

returned to Miss Lombard's side in time to take
charge of her wraps, and before consigning her
to the care of her father, a florid, full-faced man
with mutton-chop whiskers, who was awaiting
her arrival at the depot, I had obtained her per-
mission to call.   In truth, she declared she
would never forgive me if I did not.

Was there not a delightful fatality in the circumstance that the mother of Blanche should
prove to be the Lucia Merton of whom I had
heard my father speak as one of his youthful
flames?   She was, in fact, the only woman beside his wife who had ever stirred his fancy.
He had married, as Aunt Selina told me, at the
age of twenty; but I have reason to believe that
if Lucia Merton had desired it, his nineteenth
birthday would have found his troth plighted
elsewhere.   However that may be, the son of
Arthur Lattimer — the name is my father's and
my own — was received with open arms by the
Lombard family, which, beside the parents, embraced five daughters, each in her turn as
blooming and buoyant as Blanche.   It was a

rare treat to sit at their domestic board, at
either end of which shone the round, good-
humored faces of Mr. and Mrs. Lombard
wreathed in smiles, with Blanche on my right
and Fannie on my left, and the lovely trio,
Lulu, Harriett, and little Maud, across the table.
How they laughed and poked fun at each other!
The humor, like the viands provided, was of a
substantial, hearty sort. They made me feel
completely at home in five minutes, despite the
consciousness lurking in my breast, and which I
feared my face would betray, that I loved the
eldest daughter.

Mr. Lombard was a wholesale dry-goods merchant. His firm — Lombard, Little, & White —
were the selling agents for the Pimlico Mills.
He worked very hard, but spent the greater
portion of his very large income, owing to the
size of his family. Their expensive, lavish style
of living did not permit him to save anything.
I chanced to overhear these statements at the
club, after Mrs. Salisbury's ball, where I had
been dancing till past midnight with Blanche.

Two venerable *flaneurs* were interchanging over a bottle impressions regarding their acquaintances.

"Five daughters! Whew!" continued the speaker who was supplying the information. "They are a good-looking lot, though, and ought to go off pretty fast, if he has luck. I understand there is a Boston millionnaire tagging after the eldest girl."

My heart gave a painful flutter. My fears were, after all, correct. The youth whose course I had blocked in the railway station was a to-be-dreaded rival. A millionnaire, and in love with Blanche! Mr. Lombard, who was not able to lay up anything for his daughter's dowry, would welcome such a son-in-law and laugh at my pretensions. My father was well off, but a million in my own right was a sum far above what I could hope to inherit. Miserable thirst for gold, and how much more despicable when apparent in a woman! Love, pure, spontaneous love, was to be overlooked and trampled under foot for the sake of paltry riches. O Blanche!

4

Blanche! I had given you credit for a depth of
nature inconsistent with the discarding of the
affection of an honest heart to obtain a couch of
splendor.   Farewell forever.

But no.   I was premature.   I reasoned without proofs.   There was nothing to show that
she I worshipped was about to become affianced
to another.   The sweet experience of the evening just flown came back to me to soothe my
spirit.   I could see her as she stood in the
lustre of the ball-room, splendid in cream color
with pink bows, talking to four admirers in
the same breath.   Her eyes sparkled with excitement; the flush of the peach was upon
her cheeks, and her coral lips trembled with
laughter.   I had approached and added my
quota of sugared compliment and audacious
badinage to the conversation.   She giggled
convulsively at my words, and presently permitted me to carry her off to the dancing-
room.   I was not blind to the fact that her
figure perhaps appeared cumbrous and un-
wieldy amid the mazes of the waltz, or that

her feet did not move with the fairy-like agility
of more sylph-like beings; but what rapture
I experienced a few minutes later in fanning
her blown and heated loveliness in the little
alcove which leads out from the main apartments! Did she not propose that we should
eat our supper there, and send me for filet
and salad, and afterwards for pink ice-cream?
" Be sure it is pink, for I hate lemon and
pineapple," she cried, beseechingly; and yet,
when I returned with a liberal portion of the
confection she craved, the winsome girl thought
mine, which was a delicacy known as *parfait
au café*, looked nicer, and consented, upon due
importunity, to taste a spoonful of the same.
In return, she insisted that the other half of
a luscious jelly-cake on her plate should be
transferred to my lips; and when in the en-
deavor to accomplish this feat I dropped a
bit of the dainty on her dress, she gave
a hilarious little shriek, accompanied by the
phrase, " *You horrid, clumsy thing!*" Once
more did my heart thrill with joy at the sound

of these accents of maiden ecstasy. Was it
for nothing, forsooth, that she called me by
so spontaneous an appellation?

No, I thought, I will go home and sleep
tranquilly. With her sweet voice ringing in
my ears, I need not fear the predictions of
gossips. She shall be mine,—mine for eter-
nity! Therewith I swallowed another glass of
champagne, and left the two detractors of my
Blanche still crooning in their corner. I glided
down the silent staircase of the now deserted
club-house and sought the street. As I reached
the doorway, a cab drew up, the driver of which
I accosted.

"Ay, ay, sir, in a moment."

So saying, he descended from his perch and
opened the vehicle. A young man, armed with
a hat-box, got out and ran up the club steps.
We exchanged glances in passing. Doubtless
I was not recognized, but the cold tremor
which vibrated along my spine convinced me
that the stranger was no other than my victim
of the railway station.

"An accident," I heard him declare to the porter who met him at the door; "our train was delayed three hours."

Yes, it was he; the voice was the same. I flung myself into the cab. "Drive anywhere," I cried to the man; and it was only the latter's insinuation that I was intoxicated which aroused me to an appreciation of the absurdity of my order.

We met in the drawing-room of the Lombard house next day ; that is to say, the new-comer and myself. I entered with a step — the noiselessness of which was not premeditated — upon a scene where my presence was superfluous. I have no desire — for it is far from my wont to gloat over the misfortunes of others — to particularize regarding the situation. Suffice it to state that he whose eloquent posture I interrupted left town by the evening train, without seeing the realization of the hope which doubtless had prompted his journey. To say I was happy would be but a feeble epitome of the sensations I experienced when, after

his departure, I played cat's-cradle with Blanche
on the sofa in the waning light of the November
afternoon.

I think it was this very evening that before
retiring for the night I drew from my vest
pocket Aunt Selina's bauble and scrutinized it
with care. It was a perfect heart, save for a
trifling blemish where the slice had been glued
on by my aged relative. There were fine blue
lines permeating the surface of what closely
resembled flesh and blood, so much the more,
indeed, now that contact with my body had
given a semblance of human warmth to the
material. I pensively weighed the trinket for
some minutes in the palm of my hand, then,
sighing heavily, restored it to its hiding-place.

One morning, ten days later, I stood packing
my trunk amid the disorder of a littered apartment. My effects, which bore the traces of
more than a fortnight's sojourn from home, were
scattered in all directions. I tossed them into
their receptacle with the air of one who has
ceased to concern himself for the time regarding

personal trigness, but ever and anon a sigh escaped my lips, and I would for several minutes perambulate the chamber.

When at last the task was completed, I sought my toilet table, upon which lay a mass of heterogeneous articles reserved for further inspection. I raised therefrom in turn a half-dozen notes, all in the same handwriting; a trio of german favors, two in the form of stars and one a tinkling bell; a string, the same with which I had played cat's-cradle; a couple of bits of ribbon; two theatre checks; and a withered rosebud.

The notes were short, and contained invitations to dinner, or thanks for flowers which I had sent. I read them each twice, and, pressing my lips upon the signature of the last, arranged them in a packet, around which I tied one of the pieces of ribbon. The remaining objects I collected carefully in a small box, which I tied with the other. This done, I rang for a cab, and, having consigned the treasures to my trunk, put the finishing touches to my toilet.

There was on the table from which I had just removed these relics an envelope of some slight bulk, addressed and sealed with my crest, — a greyhound in the leash, with the motto, *cognosce occasionem.* This I now placed with deliberation in my pocket-book.

The coachman, in accordance with my directions, drew up at the Lombard mansion. Blanche was at home, and rose smilingly to greet me as I entered. So fresh and comely was her appearance, that some minutes elapsed before I could control myself sufficiently to disclose my ultimatum.

"What!" she cried, "going to-day?"

"Yes, it is imperative. Business of importance calls me home. I am a lawyer, you know, Miss Blanche, and the law is a severe taskmaster."

I spoke these words with an air of quiet decision, which yet was imbued with an appropriate flavor of disappointment at this necessary breach in our intercourse. I sucked the head of my stick and looked mournfully at the carpet.

" I am sorry, — real sorry," she said, and became grave and silent in her turn.

Her cheeks seemed flushed. I pitied the girl
from the bottom of my heart. I would have
done much at the time to blunt the edge of the
pain which I knew she was suffering, and was
to suffer. Anything short of an impassioned
avowal of love was her's to command; but that
was a step beyond which conscience would not
permit me to proceed, for I did not feel that
she was the spirit in whose companionship my
every aspiration would find content.

" Yes," I observed, making use of language
more metaphorical than was my custom when
talking with her, " we are but shuttlecocks tossed
about by fate. No one is fully able to carve out
his destiny. One moment we are wholly happy,
the next some roistering wind scatters our
schemes like ashes."

She made no reply, and as the old look of
constraint clothed her expression, I feared lest
I might be soaring above her comprehension.
By a few adroit sentences I led the conversation

into a less serious channel, and sought to free our interview from embarrassment.

My efforts were only partially successful, for the reason that I could not completely disguise the feelings of regard and friendliness I entertained toward her. I found myself expressing the hope that I should soon be able to return. As an offset to these expressions of interest, Blanche absented herself from the room a minute, and reappeared with a tobacco-pouch of tasteful design, which she had manufactured as payment for the forfeit lost to me. It was a trophy well worth possessing; one that I could point to with complacency in the future as the work of fair hands other than those of a kinswoman. I told her that I should prize her gift as among my most precious possessions.

I proceeded to take out the envelope from my pocket-book. I rose from my seat with the gestures of one about to take his leave, and, after a preliminary cough, said, —

"You must know, Miss Blanche, that I find it very difficult to tear myself away from this city. My stay here has been eminently agreeable, and for the larger portion — indeed I may say all — of my pleasure I am indebted to you. I earnestly trust we shall meet in the near future, and that in the mean time you will regard me as one of your sincere well-wishers. Pray, permit me to leave with you this slight token of regard. I wish it were of greater value. I shall allow you to examine it at your leisure." So saying I passed the envelope to her with a bow, and took my departure after a hearty handshaking.

My words had not the unfaltering flow that they present when committed to paper. The stammer of diffident youth impeded my utterance, and I was not sorry to find myself again in the cab whirling rapidly toward my hotel. Despite the general character of my regret at parting, I experienced already a certain buoyancy of spirit, a sensation, as it were, of a weight removed. I was still free, and the reflection, though but partially entertained, caused me self-congratulation. Nevertheless, I sighed once or twice with spontaneous intensity, and drawing forth my note-book once more I wrote, as a summing up of the entire situation: —

"She has a piece of my heart."

It was that which the envelope contained.

Evening saw me established in the centre of my family circle. They questioned me with interest regarding my travels, and dwelt admiringly on such details of adventure as I saw fit to relate. Aunt Selina sat knitting silently in her corner, but I could tell from her expression that she judged me aright, nor for an instant feared lest I had become entangled. A smile suggestive of confidence and pride hovered upon her lips. It was reserved for my sister Julia Pierson to probe the wound which rankled in my breast. The child, who had listened to my anecdotes with an air of what was almost disdain, saw fit to inquire in a meaning tone if I knew a Miss Blanche Lombard.

"Miss Blanche Lombard? Yes, Julia."

"Oh! You did not mention her," said the tormentor, dryly.

"We heard that you were very attentive to her," remarked Alice Maud.

"And ate ice-cream with her from the same plate," piped up little Medora.

"A man cannot speak more than once to the same girl without being reported engaged to her!" I exclaimed with indignation. "What nonsense you all talk! Miss Lombard and I are friends, — nothing more. She is a charming girl, though," I added, and perhaps I sighed, for two of my sisters tittered audibly.

But Julia Pierson sat bolt upright and frowned instead. "What will Leila Johnson say?" she inquired, piteously.

"Come, children, come!" broke in the voice of Aunt Selina. "It is time for bed. You forget that your brother is *the Knave of Hearts.*"

III.

I FOUND my friend "The Professor," so styled, not from the fact of his being an officer in any institution of learning, but because of his reputed wide information on all matters of popular interest, waiting for me as the Bar Harbor steamer reached the dock. I had written him to engage me rooms, and here he was at hand to greet me in person. I had come with the expectation of spending at least a month in this salubrious watering-place, for it was vacation time. The courts were closed, and it seemed quite useless to sit kicking my heels in my office. Besides, I had not been away from home since my return from New York in the early winter.

The journey in the steamer was delightful. I had sat on the deck far into the night, wrapped in my ulster, with a pipe and the stars as my only companions. A pair of laughing girls, whose chaperone was ensconced aft of the paddle-box with a male friend, would, I am confident, have been glad of my society, inasmuch as they strolled past me arm in arm more frequently than was necessary, and, though talking with volubility to each other, giggled consciously. But I was not drawn toward them. They were both beautiful in the physical sense of the word, and would probably have greatly attracted one whose experience of womankind was more limited; but there was not in the countenance of either a subtle something which I felt essential to her who could hope to chain my attention. I had noticed them at supper, and though aware, as my eye sped along and around the table, that save for their charms the company were commonplace, I gave them no encouragement, nor even smiled when the more winsome of the two upset her teacup in kittenish by-play. There

is such a thing as a conscience, and I was not
one to trifle in cold blood with a preference that
I could never expect to reciprocate.

So I sat and pondered alone; and the moon
rose from the water and cast a silver shadow
athwart the foaming wake. A pleasant breeze
played on the deep, sowing the fields of ocean
with dusky furrows.

Is there, then, thought I, no spirit in the vast
universe to mate with mine; no soul in whose
companionship my every aspiration would find
content? The beauty of the face, unillumined
by the light of intelligence, is to me but a wan
grace, and idle laughter jars upon my ear as the
clang of a tiresome bell. I lifted my face to the
peaceful skies and puffed pensively.

The disturbing approach of the flirtatious
young ladies again interrupted my meditations.
One of them in passing by contrived to drop her
glove, which fell within a short distance of where
I was sitting. A tittering ensued which would, I
dare say, have captivated a younger man, but
I, rising from my seat and picking up the glove,

restored it to the owner with an air which,
though completely gallant, was grave, and
adapted to convey the impression that such
coquetry was distasteful to me.

"Thank you very much!" the culprit exclaimed with polite effusion; and as the girls
resumed their promenade I could hear their
muffled laughter salute the darkness.

As a sequel to my insinuation I presently
left my seat, and deserting the after-deck of
the steamer passed through the saloon to the
weather-haunted seclusion of the bow. Upon
emerging from the glare of the cabin my eyes
at first led me to believe that I was alone, and
under this impression I sank upon a coil of
rope, and resting the back of my head upon my
clasped hands gazed up at the heavens. The
breeze was more perceptible, but not too cool
for comfort. Here I could be undisturbed and
give the rein to fancy. I chanced to lower my
eyes, — it may have been the *frou-frou* of a
skirt that occasioned my action, — but whatso-
ever the cause, they fell upon a slim and youth-

5

ful figure not many paces distant leaning against
the bulwark of the vessel.   A close-fitting ulster
betrayed the exquisite symmetry of her outline,
and the flowing monotony of this garment was
relieved by a lace scarf wound tight about her
neck, the ends of which fluttered in the breeze.
A billy-cock hat reposing upon a wealth of
curling, dark chestnut hair, cropped short, pre-
sumably during the ravages of fever, and neatly
banged, shaded a face of rare loveliness.   The
girl was gazing up at the sky with a yearning
intensity of expression which the ivory pallor of
her complexion, as seen under the beams of
night's empress, well became.   Her hands were
held behind her back, and her head was poised
a little upon one side.

I scarcely breathed, so great was my dread
lest any motion of mine should disturb the
beautiful apparition.   It gave me a thrill of
delicious pleasure to feel that we two were alone
under the glorious heavens, with the rhythmical
swash of the billows as the sole violators of the
sacred silence which appealed to both our souls.

Who was she? Whence had she sprung? Was
she some spirit arisen from the deep or descended along the starry ways, come to mock
me with a peep at the pose and poesy of the
immortals? I closed my eyes to make sure
that they were open, half troubled with the
dread lest I were dreaming; and when I
looked again the face and figure had faded
into distance.

At least so I fancied, and in the fulness of
disappointment I raised myself upon my elbow
and stared about me. Ah, there she was! She
had merely changed her position, and stood
gazing out to sea from the opposite side of the
deck. Her eyes now wandered over the water,
and she had made a visor for her sight with one
small, gloved hand. Her pale profile seemed to
me an eloquent breviary of pure and aspiring
sentiment.

Presently she lifted her glance once more to
the serene heavens, and overcome perhaps by
the burden of her thought, her gentle spirit
found expression in a sigh. Then it was that

my delicate sense of honor warned me that by
the rôle of eavesdropper I was wronging my
own nature no less than the fascinating stranger,
and a cough falling upon the stillness informed
her that she was not alone. At the sound she
turned her head very slightly in my direction,
then looked away. She did not alter her pose.
Thus it was for some minutes. Then she made
a few graceful steps along the deck and entered
the saloon.

I followed her as speedily as my fine perception of propriety permitted, and had the mortification to distinguish the skirt of her ulster
disappear with a tantalizing swirl behind the
door of a state-room. I saw her no more that
night; but in the early morning, when the passengers were transferred to another steamer, we
chanced to cross the gangway at the same
moment, and a single glance assured me that
night had rather robbed her of her charms than
exaggerated their lustre, for the sunlight revealed the intelligent sparkle of her deep brown
eyes and the red lips which seemed a dewy

rosebud nestling on the cream-white surface of
her countenance. She was in the company of
a venerable-looking gentleman and his wife,
whom I judged to be merely her protectors for
the occasion, seeing that she bore no resemblance to either of them. As she turned her
head midway upon the gang-plank to interro-
gate the lady in question, her eyes encountered
mine, and a subtle tremor of my frame told me
that I had detected recognition therein. No
bold nor coquettish look was there, but something which suggested the sympathy of those
who are not wholly strangers. Once more she
sought the retirement of her state-room, nor
did I catch a glimpse of her again before the
steamer reached the landing.

As I have previously observed, the Professor
was waiting for me, and I could distinguish his
pleasant countenance peering up from the
throng which lined the quay, — a throng where
youth and beauty stood allied. A large pro-
portion of the feminine element were here as-
sembled, in all the variegated attractiveness of

summer attire, anxious to note the latest arrivals; while the occasional young men of the place,

" Rari nantes in gurgite vasto,"

meandered through their midst, statuesque in knickerbockers.

So pleasing a spectacle would doubtless have appealed strongly to the ordinary worshipper of womanhood, but I must needs confess that in me this phalanx of loveliness aroused no subtler an emotion than the artistic homage which every gallant soul delights to offer on the altar of the gentler sex. My outward glance, though dazzled, dwelt neither here nor there. Conscious as I may have been that a line of beautiful eyes were riveted upon my person, perhaps in some cases with not un-flattering emphasis, I sought not to focus my own in any one direction, but followed my friend the Professor with an air of complete, though well-bred, indifference. Only once I turned my head, and then it was behind my shoulders, as if to catch a glimpse of the file of passengers still waiting to disembark.

The Professor was in his happiest mood. An authoritative and thoroughly conversant frequenter of the place, he was the person of all others to have at one's right hand upon arrival, and he hastened to supply me with sundry bits of information adapted to set me on the right track, as he called it.

"I have been here for years, and know all the ropes. Put yourself in my hands, my dear fellow, and you will be all right. Now, don't go and start anything in a hurry. Keep your head cool for a day or two, until you 've had time to look round a bit. The woods are full of them, and ten to one, if you go it blind, you will make a mistake."

"Thanks. I shall remember," I answered, perhaps a little nettled withal at his assumption of superiority.

"Do you see that quiet-looking girl with the sunflower in her hat ? She 's been engaged four times. You would n't think it, would you? I tell you it 's wonderful how they keep their looks. Any one might imagine perfectly well

she was on the sunny side of twenty. It's a
wicked world. But perhaps," continued the
Professor, "you're not going in for that style
of thing. Suit yourself. It's liberty hall, you
know, and no one is obliged here to do anything
he does n't want to."

"I mean to keep pretty quiet," said I.

"There, now," he observed, without heeding
my remark, "is a girl who might fill the bill,
I fancy. This is her first season here, and she's
catching the step pretty fast. If it were n't that
I'm occupied in another quarter, I should almost feel disposed to try my own hand in that
direction. Holloa! do you know her?"

This interrogation was caused by the bow
of marked cordiality which I bestowed on the
young lady in question, for as my eyes followed
the direction of my friend's glance they encountered the buxom face of Blanche Lombard,
under the shadow of an enormous muslin shade-
hat trimmed with pink roses. The recognition
between us was swift and mutual. Her smile of
undoubted pleasure was followed by a faint blush

and a coolness of demeanor which prompted me
to throw into my bow as much as was possible
that was brotherly and kind.

"Oh, yes. I know her quite well. She's
from New York, and a nice girl," I answered.

"All right," said the Professor. "If you are
tired, and want something new, what do you say
to the one standing next to her? She's a good
deal the same style, excepting the color of her
hair. 'You pays your money and you takes
your choice,' as the poet says."

I was silent for a moment.

"My dear fellow, neither of those girls has a
particle of soul in her face. I tell you what,
Professor, I'm weary of the flesh-and-blood
type of beauty. What I'm looking for is a
woman with expression in her countenance, —
a woman who is intelligent, and can appreciate
something beside nonsense."

He looked at me for a moment with an air
of surprise.

"Well, well! why did n't you say so before?
There are all sorts down here. You've only to

speak up and you 'll be answered. So it 's soul
you want, is it?" he continued. " I guess I shall
have to trot you up to little Fluffy Price. She
was complaining the other day that none of the
men have souls. You 'll find plenty of soul, my
dear boy, if that 's all you are worried about."

The Professor chuckled at his own humor,
and slapping me paternally on the back, began
to murmur *sotto voce* the words of a favorite
ditty of the hour: —

> "Some day, some day,
> Some day I shall meet you.
> Love I know not, when or how;
> Love I know not, w-h-e-n or h-o-w ;
> O-o-nly th-i-s, only this, that once you loved me:
> O-o-nly th-i-s, I lo-v-e " —

The sound of wheels close beside us cut short
the Professor's song, and at the same moment
he uttered an exclamation of wonder and admiration. Turning my eyes, I beheld my lovely
apparition of the night before abreast of us,
driving in one of the hotel vehicles, in company with her aged escorts. The Professor
glanced at me with suspicion.

"Who's that girl?"

"I have no idea."

"Did n't she come on the same steamer as you?"

"I think very likely."

"'Think very likely'? Come, now, you can't fool me. Confess at once that you had her to yourself all last evening."

"But I did n't. I never spoke to her in my life."

I proceeded to say that she had remained in her state-room all save a few minutes of the entire journey.

The Professor seemed thoughtful, and I noticed that he looked at his watch once or twice with an air of annoyance.

"I promised to go on a picnic this afternoon," he said, somewhat ruefully. "It's against my rule, but I wanted to oblige some one. See here, why don't you take my place? They'd be tickled to death to have a new arrival, and I've got some sketching that I shall be glad to finish."

I answered that I could not think of de-
priving him of so pleasant an entertainment,
and after due inspection of my rooms we
parted. Instinct told me that I had no time
to lose, and having doffed my travelling costume for more becoming attire, I repaired to
the particular hotel which I had been informed
was the centre of social activity. The piazza
was a scene of much gayety and bustle, and
it required some minutes of search to discover
the whereabouts of Blanche Lombard among
the bevy of girls that were there congregated.
To her I devoted ten minutes' conversation, in
which space of time I am confident of having
nipped in the bud any preconceived ideas on
her part of a continuation of the winter's relations. I was extremely friendly, and inquired
earnestly concerning her health and that of her
family. We compared our impressions of the
scenery of the place and its manners and cus-
toms. I should have been pleased to tell her
that the tobacco-pouch had been of great service to me, but for the fear lest she might

misconstrue such a remark; and in order to
avoid all danger of a misunderstanding in regard to our position, I appeared unable to
recall at first one or two of the most interesting episodes during our former intimacy. I
noticed that by degrees the light in her eyes
waned, and an expression of cold reserve settled upon her features. I slipped away presently, with the remark that I hoped to see her
often during my stay.

I entered straightway the office of the hotel,
and cannot say I was surprised to find the
Professor bending over the register.

"Holloa!" he said, as I thrust my head
into juxtaposition with his; "is that you? I
am looking to see if my cousin has arrived.
He was expected to-day."

I laughed incredulously, and glancing down
upon the open page saw that the Professor's
index-finger rested just below three names, the
perusal of which caused me an exquisite thrill.

Thomas Goldsmith and wife, Philadelphia.
Miss May Corcoran, Philadelphia.

"It's too bad, Professor," said I, "you're obliged to go to that picnic. I should like to have had a quiet chat with you."

He was stroking his chin thoughtfully. He turned to me with a mysterious wink, and remarked, —

"When you have had my experience of these things you will discover that it is n't always the sickest child who does n't get well. There's nobody to introduce you."

After which Parthian shaft he waved his hand at me by way of a farewell, and started off on the dog-trot.

I sought the piazza again, and settling myself in a comfortable chair apart from the throng, proceeded to inscribe my note-book as follows: —

No. 2.   May Corcoran.
Residence, Philadelphia.
Brunette, rare intelligence, deep nature, speaking eyes.

MEMORANDA.

Is visiting Bar Harbor with aged relatives (probably). Wears the look of a woman in search of happiness of which she has dreamed, but never experienced.

I lighted a cigarette and abandoned myself to reverie.

"Bowser," I said at length, addressing an employee of the hotel whom I had heard others accost by that name, "is there a spare canoe I can have for this evening?"

"At what hour, sir?"

"A quarter before eight."

It was now just three o'clock. I resumed my seat and sat patient, but alert, for another hour. The piazza by this time had become almost vacant. Its occupants had scattered in the pursuance of various expeditions, and only a bunch of matrons and a stray couple or two remained upon the scene.

Suddenly I saw her who was mistress of my thoughts — no other than the charming May Corcoran — step quietly from the threshold and pass down the steps of the hotel. She had exchanged her ulster and billy-cock hat for a trig blue-flannel suit and a little round hat with a loon's wing laid along the side, — a simple attire, but singularly becoming to her

style of beauty.   Just below her throat she
wore a deep red rose, which matched in shade
the sun-umbrella carried across her shoulder.
Her hand held a book that to my thinking
resembled some poet's work in the fashion of
its binding.   She passed but a few yards from
where I was sitting, and, though she did not
look in my direction, I felt conscious that she
realized my presence.   I caught a glimpse of
her face, and read thereon the same tale of exalted sentiment which had appealed to me the
evening before.

I saw her pursue the bend of the road, and
become lost to my observation.   With the careless air of one who saunters merely to kill time,
I left the piazza and followed in her footsteps.
A few moments sufficed to screen me from the
scrutiny of the hotel, and to reveal again her
graceful figure in the near distance, stepping
along the highway.   Not once did she turn
her head, but something told me that she
knew I was behind.

For nearly an hour she continued her prog-

ress. Little by little the scene changed, and
erelong the way began to lead upon one side
of the wooded banks of a brook which flowed
prattling over the stones. I could perceive her
skipping with spritelike agility from rock to
rock, when sometimes in the joy of her pure
heart she forsook the path rough with the roots
of gnarly trees for the margin of the stream. I
ever followed after, happy in the ardor of pur-
suit, and saw with increasing pleasure the rocks
transformed to bowlders, and the water grow
hoarse and foamy with its struggles.

At last, upon emerging around a bend in the
course of the valley, I beheld her close at hand,
resting against a smooth, sloping surface, at a
spot where the volume of water lay tranquil
and black in the embrace of a natural basin, —
a breathing-space as it were between the leap-
ings of the torrent. The book lay open upon
her lap, but she was not reading. Her eyes
strayed toward the western sky, already saffron
with the glow of the setting sun.

With nervous yet resolute step I advanced

6

in her direction, pausing now and again to catch the varied effects of the scenery. At length I halted just above where she was sitting, and stood resting on my cane, surveying the placid pool. Her eyes were fixed upon the pages of the open volume.

I made a step downward to the side of the rock against which she was leaning, and raising my hat with consummate politeness, said, —

"You will, perhaps, permit me to allude to the strong love of the beautiful in Nature that seems to possess us alike. If I am not mistaken, I have the honor to address her whose seclusion last evening it was my misfortune to invade. I trust you will accept the sincere, if tardy, compunction that I offer."

"Oh, sir," she replied, in a voice that seemed to me laden with the perfume of an old-time romance, "it is I who was to blame, if my bearing on that occasion suggested reproach. Are not the stars and the sea and the silver moon free for all to gaze upon who will?" She looked up at me with quiet dignity.

I think she had little conception of the poetic cadence of her words, but for me they opened a new vista of happiness. I thanked her for the considerate light in which she saw fit to regard my intrusion.

"Is not this exquisite!" I added, pointing with my cane up the long valley where we could see through the rifts in the lindens the twisting current tinged with the pink of the dying day. "I am one to whom the beauties of Nature are an unceasing source of pleasure."

She did not reply to my observation, but I could see that the play of her eyes followed the sweep of my stick.

"Are you, like myself, a stranger in these parts?" I queried.

"Yes. I have never been to Bar Harbor before. You are right," she added, "it is very beautiful. I asked my friend to tell me the prettiest walk, and she directed me to Duck Brook. This, I suppose, is Duck Brook."

I was silent in turn.

"Are you to be here some time, Miss — is not your name Corcoran? Excuse me for my boldness in asking. But something prompted me upon arrival to make inquiries as to who you might be."

She blushed a little, though I fancy hers was one of those pale complexions where the blood, however swift it may surge in the veins, rises but faintly to the surface.

"Yes, that is my name. As to my length of stay, I cannot tell. Indeed, I scarcely know why I am here. I was at Cape May three days ago. My friend Mrs. Goldsmith said she was going to Bar Harbor, and would I go also? Why not? thought I; and here I am."

I had tossed a small twig into the pool, and watched it whirled about by the relentless current.

"It is strange to think how largely we are the victims of circumstance," I observed. "Our destiny is determined for us much as that leaflet is borne along by the stream."

My words seemed for the first time to cause her genuine interest. She sighed gently and said, —

" That is deeply true." She continued presently, " I have known all my life what it is to struggle against fate."

" Indeed ! "

But I believe my manner conveyed the sympathy which was lacking in the word I employed.

" Yes," she said, dreamily, " I am quite alone in the world. I am an orphan."

She gazed into distance, and the twilight which transfigured her countenance showed also a tear drop glistening on her cheek.

" Poor girl ! " I murmured.

My expression seemed to arouse her to a sense of the unconventionality of her confession.

" You must think me very peculiar to talk to a complete stranger in this manner."

" By no means," I responded, venturing to seat myself on the rock. " Besides, I do not feel as if we were wholly strangers, Miss Corcoran."

"No? We have never met before, surely?"

"I believe not. But there are certain persons whom on a short acquaintance one feels as if one had known for a lifetime."

She did not reply at once, and then her words were rather in continuation of her autobiography than a commentary on my speech.

"My summers have largely been spent at fashionable resorts, where it was impossible to form satisfactory friendships. There is so much that is formal and heartless in the society of those places. I have heard that here it is allowable to meet one's fellow-creatures without artificiality and upon a basis of mutual confidence."

"I am one of those, Miss Corcoran, who put no belief in the popular fallacy that friendships between the sexes are out of the question. It seems to me that those who take this view deprive themselves of one of the most delightful of human joys. The society of a high-souled and intelligent woman is my idea of thorough happiness."

She tossed a pebble into the water and gazed down at her boots, which, though fashioned for climbing, were of small size.

"You have not told me your name yet. I fear that I have been making all the confidences."

I answered that it was Arthur Lattimer; that I was from Boston, and a bachelor, come hither for repose after the excitements of the winter.

"I, too, have had a season of much gayety," she responded. "What a pleasure it is to be once more in communion with Nature; to breathe the pure, invigorating air, and feast the eyes, jaded with false attractions, on the real beauty of such a scene as this! But it is time for me to be moving in the direction of home, as the sun is already below the tops of the pine-trees."

We pursued the way together, each fascinated, as it seemed to me, by the personality of the other. I found her a rarely appreciative and sympathetic listener, a woman full of most lofty and suggestive ideas regarding the vital questions of human interest. As we sauntered along in the dusk of the approaching evening the noise of a buckboard freighted with a chorus of blithe spirits obliged us to hug the footpath to escape the cloud of dust that rose from its wheels. I recognized the Professor ensconced between two young ladies, one of whom I perceived to be Blanche Lombard. The flush of self-congratulation I felt glow upon my cheek was tempered by the consciousness, which I realized, of the gulf that lay between Blanche and me. I had loved her once with a genuine and unfaltering fervor, and yet how vastly inferior her most salient charm compared with those of her who walked beside me! This reflection for a short spell saddened my brow, and was the occasion of a query from the pale beauty as to why I was so pensive.

" 'T is nothing," I answered, " but one of those transient clouds, which, whether we will or no, are apt to dim the noontide of complete happiness. Will you not," I went on to say, " allow me the pleasure of taking you out in a canoe after tea? The moon will be superb."

She acquiesced, and just then we reached the hotel. It was a proud moment for me to be her escort up the steps and through the cluster of admiring youths about the door.

"Shall I bring my banjo?" she asked, as we were about to part.

"By all means," I murmured.

I was hastening to my rooms, lost in blissful reverie, when the whistle of the Professor caused me to halt. He came running up and put his arm through mine.

"Do you know you've struck one of the most inveterate flirts in the whole of Philadelphia?"

"Well," said I, "if I come to grief, I cannot say that I was not warned, Professor."

Before leaving my apartment for the evening meal I transferred to my note-book the tenderest memories of the conversation of the afternoon. " I have known all my life what it is to struggle against fate. I am quite alone in the world, and am an orphan."

Is there a sweeter pleasure to be imagined

than that of floating under a harvest moon
with one you love? The paddle's blade parting the bosom of the dark water seems a
mysterious agency, so silent and swift is the
motion of the tiny craft, gliding along the
shores of the wooded islands, vast patches of
shadow upon a silver sea. Now and again
the ripple of voices stealing over the distance tells of other spirits partaking of a
kindred happiness, and the tinkling melody
of an occasional stringed instrument charms
the ear. The drops glisten like jewels upon
the trailing fingers of the sweet voyager re-
clining in the bow, with face upturned to the
serenity of the heavens, where Luna climbs
through diaphanous flint-blue clouds or rides
at last in untroubled splendor.

We spoke but little. Intuition warns the intelligent soul that silence is at times the most
agreeable companionship. Miss Corcoran held
across her lap her dainty banjo, and once or
twice a note of plaintive soliloquy fell upon the
stillness.

"Sing, please," I murmured.

"Ah, no! I cannot. It is too lovely."

. We shot out farther to seaward, where the yachts lay at anchor, like bats of huge and grotesque proportions. A breeze from the deep ruffled the surface and caused the skiff to sway with gentle undulations. A few sweeps of the paddle carried us under the lee of an island, and again we were at rest upon a tranquil, glittering flood.

"Is it not exquisite?" she whispered, as it were, breathless with the intensity of her emotions. "See what a broad track the moon makes. It seems almost as though it were a golden path that led to heaven."

"I once wrote a poem on that subject, Miss Corcoran."

"Did you? Oh, please recite it to me!"

"I fear I cannot remember it. Let me see. Perhaps I can recall the prelude." I was silent a moment, and then, in the impressive, clear tone which is at my disposal, began as follows: —

"''T was a night of which the glory
  Would have thrilled the meanest soul, —
  If e'er shadows of the night,
  Mellowed by that tender light,
  Have the power to distil
  From a heart which love conceals,
  Struggling with its own sweet will,
  All the latent joy it feels ;
  Or a heart of stone impress
  With a melting tenderness.

"' Sparkling in the midnight splendor,
  Close beside the cliff-girt shore
  Lay a little rocky isle
  Wooing all the stars to smile,
  And the moon to kiss, which, setting
  O'er a silent glassy sea,
  Charmed the fishers to forgetting
  Life's austere reality,
  In their huts on shore asleep,
  Just where ocean could not creep.' "

" Oh, do go on ! " she cried, as I paused at the completion of this stanza.   " It is beautiful ! "

I replied that I had forgotten the precise language of the rest.

" Besides, the poem is too long to repeat.   It is the story of a fisher-maiden whom her affianced lover had forsaken.   She was in the habit

of rowing out from the mainland to the island,
whence she would gaze out to sea with the hope
of catching a glimpse of his returning sail.
Somebody had told her, too, that the souls of
faithless lovers inhabit the moon, and it came
into her mind that by following the glittering
wake she would at last greet her sailor-lad once
more.

> " ' Fastened by a rope that gleamed
> Like a braided silver strand,
> Her slight skiff lay all at rest
> On the tranquil ocean's breast.
> The wide heaven seemed to glisten,
> Touched by her grief uncontrolled ;
> Every star stooped down to listen
> To the tale the maiden told ;
> While the pitying Pleiad's creeping
> Up night's vault wept golden weeping.' "

" How touching, Mr. Lattimer ! "

" She apostrophizes the moon and asks the
golden planets' protection : —

> " ' Take me, take me, precious light,
> To thy mystic, jewelled cave
> Down through the still ocean floor,
> And I 'll be thy trusty slave
> In the deep for evermore.' "

" It is very poetical," said the sweet, yearning voice of Miss Corcoran.

" In the next verse she explains her hope," said I.

> " ' Those who their true vows have broken
>   In thine orb are said to dwell.
>   When the fates his life-threads sever,
>   And my lover sleeps forever,
>   Haply I shall find him there ;
>   Banish his repentant tears,
>   Win his pardon by a prayer,
>   Or remorse of future years
>   Calm by love so deep.   Sweet light,
>   Let me go with thee to-night.

> " ' From the barren rock uprising,
>   To her feet the skiff she drew.
>   The rough oars she deftly plied,
>   And her bark flew o'er the tide,
>   Bearing her far from the shore
>   Of her childhood's misery,
>   Until it seemed nothing more
>   On the wide illumined sea
>   Than a speck of cloud or mist
>   By both sky and ocean kissed.' "

"And what became of the poor child?" asked my companion, for I was silent now.

" She was never heard of again. Neither she

nor the boat was ever found. There is a legend, though, among the fishermen of the place that on calm summer nights,

> " ' When the stars in countless cluster
> Peep from heaven, and the lustre
> Of the moon is at its prime,
> A pale maiden museth still,
> Just as in the olden time,
> On the isle, and seems to fill
> Night with peace ; and well they know
> In her hour no storm will blow.' "

"What a truly exquisite poem. Why have you never published it?"

"I sent it to the editor of a magazine once, and it was returned. In my mortification I cast the manuscript into the fire. What I have recited to you is from memory."

"It seems to me very beautiful. I have," she observed, in a tone of exquisite modesty, "written verses occasionally myself."

"Ah, pray give me the felicity of listening to some of them."

"Not to-night. They would sound vapid after yours. Some other time," she continued, perceiving the importunity of my manner. " Paddle a little, Mr. Lattimer.   I think we are drifting too far from home."

By a few turns of my sinewy wrist I sent the canoe flying in the direction she desired.   She was silent for some minutes, lost apparently in the plenitude of her fancy.

" What, Mr. Lattimer," she asked at length, " is your definition of love ? "

I answered with my customary ready pertinency: "Love is the silent sympathy which vibrates from soul to soul."

"What a charming description!" she murmured; " that is just what it is, — silent. I cannot endure the conception of love that delights in noise.   True love seems to me in its essence a dreamy passion, a holding of hands in the darkness, so to speak, — a sitting side by side with a finger on the lips.   Do you understand what I mean, Mr. Lattimer, or is my interpretation too vague ? "

" No, no ! " I cried, "your language is delicious.   Would that there were more in the world who feel as you do. We live in a literal age, and life is shorn of genuine poetry. All, all are gone, — the ghosts and fairies, the hob-goblins and elves, the sprites and witches, — even the devil himself."

" Yes; and where, too, are the bards and min-strels, the troubadours and tourneys, and the gallant knights, who, for the love of their gentle ladies, slew the dragons who belched forth fire from their brazen throats?"

"Gone too; and with them the silken lad-ders and stolen kisses, the precious locks of hair and secret billets, — even the cruel parent, and chaise-and-four to Dover. Not one is left. Love's cottage, that nightmare of ambitious mothers, is marked 'To let,' and I hear an enterprising speculator is going to pull it down and build an apartment-house, with all the modern improvements, on the site. In their stead we have the reporter and the photog-rapher and the manager, to show us life as it really is. But yet," I added, in a tone of quiet pathos, "there are ever a faithful few to

7

bewail the degeneracy of the many, ever a heart here and there where the sacred fire burns with the heat of the ages."

Her response was a sigh so exquisitely melodious that the paddle stood idle in my hand. She touched the strings of her banjo, and as once more I urged the skiff over the water, these were the words she sang, — words that I have never heard before nor have heard since, but the memory of which fills my heart even to-day with a thrill of joy that is half pain : —

> " A maiden stood on a dreary ledge
> And gazed at a foaming sea;
> Her eyes were brown as the slippery sedge
> Which the wild waves tossed in their glee.
> Her eyes were brown, but were moist with grief,
> And she moaned to the billowy brine, —
> ' The life of my true love is thine, cruel thief,
> And naught do I care for mine !
> The life of my true love is thine, c-r-r-u-el th-i-e-f,
> And n-a-u-ght do I c-a-a-re for mine ! '

> " The sea, with the growl of an angry bear,
> Swept over the dreary ledge,
> And mingled the brown of the maiden's hair
> With the brown of the slippery sedge;

But a woman's voice that rejoiced in its grief
    Outsped the roar of the brine, —
' The life of my true love is thine, cruel thief,
    And naught do I care for mine !
The life of my true love is thine, c-r-r-u-el th-i-e-f,
    And n-a-u-ght do I c-a-a-re for mine ! ' "

" Ah," I exclaimed, as the last note of her sweet voice died away on the night air, " what a delicious thing ! so spirited and yet so weird and suggestive ! Not a word wasted ! Where did you obtain it ? "

" It was written by a friend of mine," she replied, with a modesty as delectable as her dreamy tone.

" I can see the whole scene," said I. " It stands out vividly before me, — the desolate, wind-blown ledge, the wan maiden with dishevelled hair, and eyes salt with tears. The huge waves come tumbling in and sweep her from her foothold, and tangle her tresses with the fronds of the treacherous sea-weed. Then, when it seems as if the pitiless destroyer had triumphed, a beautiful white arm rises for an instant above the foam of the surges, and a cry

of despair, which is exultation, outvies the roar
of the tempest!"

She thanked me for my appreciation of her
song, and thenceforward we were almost silent.
With a due and delicate perception that the
point had been reached in the interchange of
sympathy where reaction is liable to occur, or
at least where there is no likelihood of a stricter
tension of the cords of feeling, I now turned
the canoe's head toward shore, and we were
landed just as the steel-blue clouds, grown
more dense and cumbrous, threatened to conceal the visage of the moon.   We parted at
the foot of the stairs leading to her apartment
without words, but interchanging that cordial
pressure of the hand which tells of emotions
which language seldom formulates except to
mar.

Next morning, after breakfast, we were tin-
typed, and, since the previous day's experience
had given me assurance, I permitted the Professor, whose eloquent look of reproach went
to my heart, to become the third figure in our

final sitting. As we posed at Miss Corcoran's feet, upon either side, our fair companion found some difficulty in assuming an attitude that promised to be both appropriate and effective. It was at the height of her uncertainty that the Professor observed, with his well-known air of jocose yet genuine gallantry, —

"*Il faut souffrir pour etre belle.*"

"Say, rather," I exclaimed upon the instant, glancing respectfully but with sentiment in the direction of my fair *protégée*, — "say, rather, *il faut etre belle pour souffrir ;* for who truly can suffer so keenly as she who sees mankind in hopeless adoration at her feet? Even their misery is less poignant than the harrowing pity which scalds her tender bosom."

A sad but beautiful smile was the reward of my gentlemanly antithesis to the Professor's flippancy ; and I think that he must himself have perceived the futility of his efforts, for erelong he pleaded an engagement, and left Miss Corcoran and me once more alone.

It boots not to dwell with prolixity on the

events of the ensuing four weeks, which, however teeming with variety for the parties immediately concerned, would haply strike the casual
reader as monotonous.

We sought not the approbation of observers
at the time, but, careless of invidious comments,
found an ample happiness in the unreserved
companionship of each other.   It was our wont
to sally forth upon expeditions calculated to
consume the larger portion of the day, and the
star of twilight would often be our guide upon
the homeward path.   We climbed to the top of
the neighboring mountains and made explora-
tions of the bold, impressive coast, pausing at
mid-day beneath the protection of some natural
shelter, to share the cold chicken and dough-
nuts which we conveyed [1] for luncheon from the
hotel.   Then, stretched at ease upon a grassy
bank or along some smooth ledge, we whiled
away the hours in the discussion of a wide

[1] "'Convey,' the wise call it. 'Steal!' A fico for
the phrase." — *The Merry Wives of Windsor*, Act I.
scene 3.

range of topics, until warned by the sloping shadows of the approach of evening. I have reason to believe that May made me the confidant of every circumstance in her sweet life, and I in turn told her those thoughts and facts regarding myself which I intrust only to those whose personality is, as it were, a portion of my being. In the course of our reflections upon the nature of love, she gave me to understand that the first bloom of her heart had been bestowed upon one who proved faithless. The breaking of her engagement, though her own deed at the last, had been consequent upon the cruel neglect of him in whom she had put a trust which was without limit. The searing marks of this sorrow still burned in silent hours, and those who knew her best declared her much altered in appearance. Never until the present summer had she felt any return of her old-time vivacity.

All this she told me one afternoon, just at dusk, under the influence of a young moon streaking the pale sky. We were sitting close to the water, and after the free, untrammelled methods common to us at such times, she had borrowed my white flannel skull-cap, that her head might rest more comfortably against the bowlder; while I in turn was adorning hers with a coronal of sea-mosses gathered from the beach.

It is a strange but melancholy truth, we are not always masters of our thoughts at moments when they should be of the most disinterested character. Deep as was my sympathy for the sufferings undergone by this gentle soul, I could not abstain from recalling my own reflections the night before, when, under the sway of an analytic mood, I had taken out and scrutinized with care the composition heart that once belonged to Aunt Selina. With all the wealth of sentiment I entertained for May Corcoran, was not I, too, among those whose affections no longer wear the beautiful guise that is the benison of inexperience? I, too, could no longer offer to another the first and most exquisite bloom of my love. I still worshipped, — wor-

shipped indeed with a passion which was perhaps
more discriminating and intelligent than that of
former days; but yet the lurking consciousness
was mine of a certain impoverishment, as though
a thief had invaded the sanctuary of my bosom
during the still hours of night and stolen some
precious jewel. I had for an instant the previous
evening caught a glimpse of this bitter truth,
which now again passed through the chamber
of my brain with the stealthy stride of a spectre.
No sooner had it vanished than the torrent of
my love flowed once more with impetuosity
through my breast; but some subtle power had
tinged its waters with an icy coldness that almost
against my will tempered the ardor of my subsequent words. It is to them that I must refer
for the elucidation of the scene that ensued.

"Miss May," said I, for she had finished her
narration, and sat looking out over the sea with
a pitiful, suffering gaze, "the first time I saw you
I was convinced that you had been the victim
of a subversive sorrow. Even then," I added,
"my deep sympathy, which brims over to-day

at the mention of your grief, was awakened;
for not only did the indescribable affinity exist-
ing between your soul and my soul — an affinity
that I think you will not disclaim after the intimacy of these weeks — reveal to me your secret,
but also because I myself am not wholly a
stranger to such an experience as you have
described."

"Ah," she replied, with a glance of tender
interest, "it pains me to hear it, for a heart so
warm and trusting as yours must have been
sorely smitten."

"You must not mistake my meaning," said
I, quietly. "Mine is not an instance where
the deliberate faithlessness of one in whom I
had trusted caused a wound. There are, perchance, those who would lay at my own door
the source of my sorrow. In short, the enthusiastic blindness of youth led me at one time to
pour out my heart's fresh passion at the feet of
one who, though beautiful in person, proved to
lack those requisites which I yearned to encounter in that spirit in whose companionship

my every aspiration would find content. Would
to Heaven, Miss May, you and I had met before
the fell stroke of destiny mildewed the blossom
of both our loves."

I was silent, and with mechanical gesture
tossed now and again in the air Aunt Selina's
composition heart, which I had taken from my
pocket. My companion still gazed seaward
with an aspect where intensity had begun to set
its seal in contradistinction to the hopelessness
of her recent expression.

I balanced the bauble upon my open palm
and surveyed it pensively. Upon her asking
what I was examining with so much interest,
I made no response for an instant, and then
with a quiet sigh placed the treasure in her
hand. My eyes at this moment met hers, and
reading therein a secret, which yet had not
been a secret to me for many days, I would
fain have knelt upon the bare rock and asked
leave to hold forever the white taper fingers
which brushed against mine. But a subtle
power restrained and prompted words which

fell far short in meaning of the phrases I should
otherwise have employed.

"That is merely a keepsake which I happen
to have discovered in my pocket, but which
seems to me symbolic of our mutual condition.
A glance will show you the device is that of a
human heart, — a heart which bears upon its
surface the imprint of suffering, the maceration
of bitter experience. See," I added, bending toward her with an air of tenderness, "where the
knife has sliced its way through the blue veins,
leaving the flesh sore to the most trivial touch."

"Yes," she answered; "it is, indeed, an eloquent commentary on the misery of life. But,"
and here she turned and looked at me with
gentle yearning, "the kind sympathy of friends
does much to alleviate and poultice the most
sensitive wound."

"Ah!" I exclaimed, "it gives me an unutter-
able joy to hear from your own lips that my
efforts at consolation have not been completely
in vain. Yes, Miss Corcoran, I think I may
claim, without incurring the imputation of too

great assurance, that my sympathy of the past
few weeks has contributed largely to lessen the
desolation under which your spirit labored
when first we met. Not," I added, with emphasis, " that the wound has wholly healed,
for so complete a result we must leave, my
dear young lady, to time, the great physician;
but still, I believe that our mutual influence
has been to invigorate the weary soul of one
another, rather than foster the growth of a
pent-up grief."

" Indeed it has," she murmured; and her
eyes fell diffidently, as though unable to bear
the penetrating gaze of mine. Had I obeyed
the momentary instincts of my bosom, I
should have clasped her in my arms then and
there.

" I even believe," I went on to say, " that the
time is not far distant when, alike to your heart
and mine, will return the pristine joy of the
days which were before we knew what it was
to have loved, — a joy wearing not perhaps the
fleckless bloom of unsophisticated youth, but

rather the serene front of happiness tempered
and refined in the furnace of adversity.   But
however that may be, — and who indeed can
say what fate has in store for any one of us? —
the memories of this summer's experience will
be a source of sweet reminiscence to both you
and me.   Let me at least declare, upon my own
behalf, that I recognize in you a being far
removed above the ordinary plane of humanity,
— a woman whose pure and ennobling estimates
of life's meaning will be precious companions
to me during the remainder of my existence.
I have made a friend whose constancy I can
never call in question, and whose nature is in
exquisite sympathy with my own.   To say that
I regret being obliged to leave Bar Harbor
to-morrow would convey but a faint expression
of my feelings.   I deplore the necessity which
calls me away, and thereby sunders the delightful relations of the past month.   It is
another instance of the rigor of those laws to
which all mortal life is amenable."

"What!" she said, as I became silent, "going

to-morrow? I am indeed grieved to hear it."
She paused an instant, and then continued
quietly: "You can feel assured that the kind
words you have spoken are not unappreciated,
however in excess of the truth as regards my
attributes. The friendship to which you refer
will be very precious to me, and"—

She did not finish her sentence, for the falter-
ing of her voice betrayed the intensity of her
emotion. In a chance nervous movement of her
hand the heart given me by Aunt Selina fell
upon the rock and was broken. Another section was divided from the main portion, leaving
only a complete half of the original bauble.
Stooping down, I picked up the débris, assuring
her that the accident was of but trifling importance. Then with a smile of quiet, composed
friendship I asked her to accept the piece as a
slight token of my regard.

"It is," I added, "of insignificant value in
itself, but may serve to call to mind pleasant
memories, if I may be so bold as to assume that
your memories of me will be agreeable."

She received the segment, which was streaked with the line of a blue vein, and put it in the little reticule at her waist. She did not speak, but I could see that she was deeply moved. So in truth was I, and for many minutes sat motionless, looking out over the dark water, upon which the mantle of evening was descending. I pitied the pale, lovely girl with all my heart, for even my intuition had not revealed the depth of the impression which I had made upon her. I should have endeavored to say something consolatory had it not been for the fear lest she might deem such words more significant than their real purport. I merely observed that all separations were painful to bear, and, after a deep sigh or two, suggested the advisability of turning our steps homeward to avoid being overtaken by the darkness.

·Early the next morning I left Bar Harbor. The Professor, who knew all, came down to the wharf to see me off. He rallied me upon the lowness of my spirits.

" Cheer up! I have had similar experiences,"

he said. "You will feel all right in a few days. It is hard, but a necessary step."

I shook my head mournfully, and grasping his hand as I stood on the edge of the plank: "Professor," I murmured, "she has a piece of my heart."

8

IV.

" MR. LATTIMER, I should like to introduce
you to Miss Virginia Langford."

I bowed to Mrs. Bellingham with an air of
well-bred complaisance, which, while expressing
complete readiness to make the acquaintance of
the young lady in question, was free from the
eagerness of extreme youth. There was a time
when such a proposition would have brought
the blush of gratified pride to my cheeks; but
I was no longer a stripling. With the accretion
of a little more flesh, — though not enough to
prejudice the proportions of my person, — a
collected dignity had become manifest in my
bearing. It required now much to throw me
off my balance. I was not easily disturbed, nor

did I give way to enthusiasm without adequate cause.

Mrs. Bellingham, at whose *musicale* I was present, conducted me through the exquisite suite of rooms thrown open for the reception of her guests. As my eye passed along the line of handsome, well-dressed women, who represented adequately the fashion of the city, I could perceive that my finished appearance excited much interest. Whispers as to who I might be reached my ear, and the half-coquettish smile which rises to the lip of beauty on the approach of a man of consummate *chic* was not infrequent. I was a stranger in Baltimore, and, save for my fascinating hostess, had no acquaintance of moment.

As we walked, Mrs. Bellingham gave me information, in her sprightly fashion, concerning certain of her visitors. The tall girl with the exquisite coloring talking to Mr. Nelson was Miss Ethel Buell, whose father was treasurer of the prosperous Patapsco Manufacturing Company. She was a great favorite. That was

Miss Rantoul in the corner, — the girl with the alabaster skin and black hair; it was she to whom the Prince of Wales had taken such a fancy a year before.

I listened to her comments with polite interest, and evinced the necessary degree of appreciation at each recital. With my wide experience of the sex I was not to be easily captivated, but neither was I a captious critic. Both Miss Buell and Miss Rantoul struck me as well-appearing young ladies, with either of whom one might pass an evening and find alike enjoyment and a theme for some enthusiasm.

"I want you, though, to meet Miss Langford," said my hostess. "I am sure you will think her very charming. This is her second winter in society, but practically her first, for poor, dear Mrs. Langford's health was so delicate last year that she carried off Virginia to the South early in February. She has lived abroad a great deal, and has quite foreign manners. So elegant and high-bred! Quite in contrast to the free-and-easy style one sees so much of

nowadays. Don't you think our American girls
are apt to be a little too informal in their ways,
Mr. Lattimer?"

"It is a great fault of the age, Mrs. Bellingham," I answered gravely. "I must confess
that I have little sympathy with that school of
deportment which relies on a lack of ceremony
as its most salient charm."

"Ah, there she is!" and Mrs. Bellingham
turned our steps towards an adjacent sofa upon
which a young lady was sitting whose demeanor
suggested to me a princess, so replete it was
with proud dignity.

The admirers, three in number, who were in
attendance, stood aside at our approach, and
Miss Langford herself arose to greet the elder
lady.

"Virginia, my dear, allow me to present to
you Mr. Arthur Lattimer. Mr. Lattimer is
from Boston."

I bowed with the air of careful gallantry,
where respect goes hand in hand with a silent
avowal of fascination.

" Miss Langford, I think that you know Miss Delano? "

" Ah, yes; she is one of my best friends. Are you a friend of hers, Mr. Lattimer? "

" I flatter myself that I am to be considered in that category."

Thus by a single phrase I had placed myself in complete sympathy with this exquisite creature ; for Miss Delano was, though not of prepossessing appearance, one of the most fashionable and wealthy girls in my native city. I was, indeed, upon terms of intimacy with her, or I should not have ventured the assertion, for breeding such as that with which I now found myself face to face would easily have seen through the gauze of imposture. Nothing is so difficult to simulate as the methods of cultivated people.

This girl had a stately and commanding presence. She stood erect, with her head thrown slightly back, revealing in their full, dazzling whiteness the swan-like neck and plump but symmetrical shoulders which were among her claims to pre-eminent beauty. Her eyes were of that pale-violet shade which, when other attributes are not incongruous, give to their possessor the mild but aristocratic aspect of the mountain deer. Every movement was distinguished for its grace, and every word she uttered was delightfully modulated, as though a harmony of refinement prevailed betwixt her body and soul.

I found myself silently according to Miss Langford that genuine applause which is the outcome of comparison. Her elegance put memory to the blush, so that I wondered how I could have become enraptured with others while so exquisite a being drew breath. This was no haphazard, boyish impulse of infatuation, but the mature deduction of manhood, with experience as a mentor.

I think that she almost instantly conceded something of the same excellence to me. Though young in years, she had indisputably seen much of life, or, more accurately speaking, of mankind, and could at a glance distin-

guish the complete cavalier from the mere tyro
or consequential nobody. After some general
conversation, by a few words, the tact of which
was admirable, she dismissed the youths in
attendance and composed herself on the sofa
for a quiet chat with me. She did not deem
it necessary to seek the seclusion of the staircase or an ante-room in order to satisfy her
vanity, nor did I for a moment think of sug-
gesting a proceeding that would not have failed
to appear to her indecorous. We both were
amply able to converse without the aid of coquettish devices, and the slight haughtiness
which, as it were, fringed her manners struck me
as a grace.

Before going to bed that night I put down
the name of Virginia Langford as number six
in my calendar of fair women. Suffice it for
the present to state that since taking leave of
May Corcoran at Bar Harbor I had been on
terms of intimacy with three other charming
girls, to each of whom I had given a piece of
my heart at parting. Three years had passed

since Aunt Selina vouchsafed me the interview which had colored the current of my existence, and I was still faithful to the estimate the old lady formed of my character. Many an hour since then I had felt a thrill of self-congratulation at the thought that I had not thrown myself away prematurely. A wedded life with one like Blanche Lombard would have checked the development of those intellectual and social charms of which I now appreciated the value, and never more than at this time, when I found myself at the feet of a woman who would be quick to recognize their existence.

No. 6. Virginia Langford.
Residence, Baltimore.
Elegant, accomplished, statuesque.
Black hair ; a light coloring ; violet eyes.

MEMORANDA.

" The expectancy and rose of the fair state,
    The glass of fashion and the mould of form."

For the benefit of those unfamiliar with the method of the courtship of a woman of so

queenly a type, let me state that, with all my
experience and might of fascination, any hope
I may have cherished of carrying her heart
by storm speedily subsided. She regarded
homage in the light of a perquisite, and un-
disguised admiration affected her for the most
part less than the onset of the raging sea, the
impassive shore. Her power of attraction was
like the baleful effulgence of a beacon light,
against the glass windows of which the bewil-
dered birds dash themselves amid the storm's
fury and drop dead. I know that such a
thought came to me as I watched the candi-
dates for her smiles succeed each other.

I saw clearly that the path to influence with
her was one from which all but the most dis-
cerning and skilful lover would be sure to
wander.   There was a long, narrow stretch
of uneventful country to be trodden, where,
however, a single false step would induce de-
struction. It was needful to satisfy her vigi-
lant sense of good taste and refinement, and
interest her intelligence, before any suggestion

of sentiment on my part would be capable of awakening aught but pity in her bosom.

I sat beside her at dinner the evening following Mrs. Bellingham's entertainment. There are some young ladies whom it would flatter to have been addressed as " Miss Virginia," but I took care to call my neighbor " Miss Langford," feeling that her delicacy would shrink from what seems to me a piece of unnecessary familiarity. May Corcoran I had almost invariably accosted as " Miss May," from a consciousness that the simple use of her cognomen would have appeared to her to smack of a formality that did not exist between us.

After an interchange of those insipidities which are the liveried forerunners of polite conversation, we touched upon a topic which brought the soul's fire to her eyes, — the world - famed debate between Webster and Hayne. Her sympathies were those of a Southern aristocrat, and in her efforts to prove the superiority of the arguments used by the champion of States' rights she fairly became roused. In her excitement the tears for an instant glittered in her eyes, and I crumbled my bread with the complacency of one who has produced an impression.

Without too marked an egotism, I gave her to understand that it was my ambition to make a name for myself, while contributing to the world's advancement, and in a few epigrammatic sentences I disclosed to her the pith of my philosophy and the themes in which I felt the keenest interest, and I was not surprised to find her tastes and views somewhat akin to my own, though less advanced, as was befitting one of her sex.

"Miss Langford," I said, in continuation of some observations on feminine education, "my opinions on this subject are of a decided character. My reverence and admiration for all that is embraced under that sweet word 'woman' — and in especial when I think of the vast and wonderful influence she has upon the creature man — is such that I cannot but deprecate the errors of a training which seeks to reduce her

to the status of a mere puppet, — a conventional
doll. I am one who believes that the advancement of the human race is contingent, to a vital
degree, on the character of her future discipline.
The elevation of the sex to which I belong is a
work meet and possible for her performance;
but provided, however, that her intelligence can
be brought into a more intimate affinity with
those exquisite sympathies which are the main-
spring of her being. Let reason walk hand in
hand with aspiration, and her triumph is secure.
Give to a due understanding of the laws of hy-
giene a portion of the prominence bestowed
upon the hymnal, and the friends of progress
will have occasion to rejoice."

I paused, and, glancing down at my plate,
impaled on my fork with pensive precision some
of the peas which embellished the *filet de bœuf*.

"Really, Mr. Lattimer." She spoke in the
tone of surprised pleasure which we are apt to
evince at the discovery in another of opinions
similar to our own. She looked at me in a
deeply interested manner, but I was not so

unsophisticated as to ascribe her intensity to any special regard for me as an individual. It was my theme, not my personality, which appealed to her imagination. " That is one of my pet theories. I feel so much — don't you? — that women, in order to retain their influence, must learn to think for themselves."

I took a sip of wine, and, coughing slightly, replied, —

" I consider individuality as the brightest star in the coronet of civilization, Miss Langford. Let that be suppressed, and humanity will languish. The ability to reason more and more accurately from cause to effect is a condition of the world's progress. I am a Spencerian to that extent, and recoil from all methods calculated to fetter the free play of the intelligence."

" I suppose you have read all Herbert Spencer, Mr. Lattimer. I am not familiar with the whole of his works, but those which I have read interested me very much. Do you not think that his philosophy has influenced greatly the present generation?"

"It is not so much his philosophy, it seems to me, as his wonderful gift of detecting the weak spots in the armor of his adversaries. He lays error bare with the cool precision of a surgeon, nor heeds the writhes of the victim. That which is becoming imprinted on the thought of the day is the flimsy fallacy of the past's deductions, upon which the philosopher has let in a flood of sunshine, rather than the system which he offers in their stead. His so-called philosophy appears to me cold and pulseless. His theory of existence suggests the gray, frigid tranquillity of a November sky. Where, for instance, does he accord aught but a chary welcome to identity, or give a due rank, among the potent forces of the universe, to the beautiful devotion, aspiring purity, and unselfish love of woman?"

"That is true, very true," she murmured; and I perceived the keen soul-thirst for the undiscernible and unattainable gleaming in her eyes.

I could have grasped her hand, — indeed, had the surroundings permitted, I think I should

have done so, — and poured out the tide of
adulating passion which swelled up to my
lips. But I was prudent in the midst of my
frenzy, and no blind puppet to the power of
infatuation. I am referring now, not to my
abstention from a declaration, but to the rare
judgment which told me that she whom I
loved was not a woman to be won merely by
the eloquence of an enthusiastic spirit. Greatly
as she would admire, and even idealize, one
whose lofty purposes and earnest thoughts
stirred her soul, yet I felt confident that she
would hesitate to link her destiny with any
save an individual whose physical traits were
also excellent. It was not beauty of face and
structure that I had in mind, though these
were advantages not to be overlooked, but
the exquisite gifts of grace, elegance, and tact,
which sit as lightly on the well-bred soul as
the foam on the sea. The body is the complement of the spirit, and Virginia Langford
suffered too keenly at the lapses of the unre-
fined, ever to give her heart where a princely

demeanor was not the concomitant of lofty
character.

And so I changed the current of the conversation, and allowed her to appreciate my
familiarity with the usages and diversions of
fashionable society. By a number of little
gallantries which are mere titillations to a complete belle, but nevertheless acceptable, I proved
that she would be justified in according to me
that footing which is granted only to equals.
The elegance — I can think of no other word —
which had characterized my attitude toward her
at the beginning of the entertainment was still
noticeable, and I ventured to add thereto a
slight flavor of sentimental interest, — a mere
soupçon, however, one of those scarcely perceptible quantities which, whether in culinary or
more momentous affairs, are available only to
an artist. How many men in my position would
have yielded to the superficial temptation of
making capital out of the mottoes to be found
in the *bonbonnières* that followed the dessert! I
might easily, by a single maladroit remark in

connection with such flippancy, have jarred the
concord established between us. To one couplet
which embodied gross and egregious flattery I
did indeed call her attention, but merely for the
purpose of expressing my distaste for so fulsome
rhodomontade. Then drawing forth a pencil I
proceeded to offer as a theme for her ingenuity
several enigmas, principally in French. With
some of these she was already familiar, but I
was glad to find that she had never seen the one
I considered the best. It was an old conceit,
worn almost threadbare in the social circle of
my native city, but graceful of its kind. I had
drawn six lines, which were presumed to repre-
sent lances, between the letters of the words
j'aime, on my dinner-card, as follows: —

$$\hat{|}\,J'\,\hat{|}\,a\,\hat{|}\,i\,\hat{|}\,m\,\hat{|}\,e\,\hat{|}$$

I passed it for her inspection, with the request
that she would solve its meaning. For some
minutes she pondered over the device, and made
several conjectures as to the interpretation.
Finally the solution occurred to her, and she

repeated the phrase in a tone where the keen satisfaction of her success was tempered slightly by the import of what the words conveyed.

J'aime en silence (*six lances*).

"It is pretty, very pretty, Mr. Lattimer," she continued.

"There is an answer which in certain circumstances would be appropriate," I said gayly, but a practised ear scarcely could have failed to detect the supplication lurking in my voice.

I handed her another design, which was a rough representation of a rat resting upon the roof of a house. It was likewise an enigma to be expressed in French, so I told Miss Langford.

This time she was compelled to confess herself nonplussed, and I wrote the explanation below the sketch, with a quiet smile.

Rassure-toi (*rat sur toit*).

"Ah," she cried, "how clever! The woman who rose to the occasion so charmingly must have been worth winning."

"But the petition must often have been

breathed without evoking so happy a response,"
I replied, with a touch of sententiousness.

" Yes," she said, breaking a bit off a macaroon
beside her plate; " but he always would have
the counsel of England's maiden queen as a
mentor, — ' If thy heart fails thee, climb not
at all.' "

The moment she had spoken the words I
could see that she repented having done so ; for,
though they were harmless enough in one sense,
an adept like myself would be swift to note the
challenge implied therein, which was made clear
to my perception as the ringing note of a genuine herald from the rampart of a castle of
strength. She was even a shade embarrassed,
— an unusual circumstance for her, — and a
frown which was half a blush shadowed her
face, just as the pink of sunset deepens into
violet.

In the case of an equally proud but less delicate woman I should have upset a wineglass at
this juncture in order to give my neighbor an
opportunity to recover her equanimity unob-

served; but fearing lest so manifest a piece of
awkwardness might offend her sensibilities, I
contented myself with calling the attention of
the company to the absurd appearance of a
young man across the table who had donned
one of the paper head-gears which *bonbonnières*
contain. It was a tissue-paper imitation of what
is known as a poke-bonnet, and the juvenile in
question, having tied the strings underneath his
chin, was eminently tickled at what he presumed
to be his comicality; whereas he bore a striking
resemblance to an insane person, to say nothing
of the discomposure of his hair. I could not
help reflecting that a year or two back I had
been guilty on several occasions of a like inanity;
and the consciousness of my present dignified
appearance, albeit the result of experience, as
contrasted with this youth's, was a source of
congratulation to me.

As soon as the laughter which this episode
occasioned had subsided, the hostess gave the
signal for the departure of the ladies, and I,
while drawing back my chair to allow Miss

Langford an abundant means of egress, bowed
profoundly and respectfully.   No vestige of anything but the address of a gallant acquaintance
was discernible in my manner, but my pulse
quickened joyfully as she swept by with queenly
dignity to see that in the meeting of our eyes
hers were troubled, and that their violet hue
suggested the misty atmosphere that veils the
tops of mountains.   Some would have been
discouraged by the seeming indifference of her
air, for she certainly did not bestow upon me
a glance that a dog would have coveted ; but a
subtle instinct, which belongs at times as well to
man as to the other sex, or it may have been
the power of perception arising from much observation, told me that I was the subject of her
reflections.   Even as frost in the silent night
splits open the chestnut burrs and reddens the
leaf of the maple, so enters love into the breast
of woman.

The passion which stirs in the heart of a man
after knowledge of life has freed him from ser-
vitude to the delusions of youth makes up in

depth for what it may lack in mere ungovernable ardor. I can confidently state that while I might readily have been exposed to the fascinations of a hundred beautiful women without feeling one sentient throb, now that love had come again, I realized his worth not less, though perhaps differently, than in the days when he chafed at the touch of the rein. I could now tolerate, and even recognize as suitable, that the eternal fitness of things should be a factor in the affairs of the heart. Love should none the less be pure, aspiring, and spontaneous; but yet rationalism ought so far to govern as to shield the soul from an alliance based wholly on transcendental considerations. Affection in a cottage no longer appealed to me with the potency of yore, nor did also, in truth, the happiness of a union with a mate whose family tree lacked the symbols of age, or whose person was not a reflex of consummate breeding. To love in the best and truest sense, the faculty of discrimination must be on the alert to woo the eternal fire in its choicest receptacle; or, indeed, the capacity for reciprocation in the highest meaning exists only where all the qualities of human excellence, both physical and psychical, are united.

The discussion of questions kindred to these — of course purely from an abstract standpoint — came to be of frequent occurrence between Miss Langford and myself. She held strenuously to the doctrine that while a girl should never marry save when her heart was controlled by the most exquisite emotion, yet a marriage dictated solely by infatuation might be an equal if not more disastrous evil. She, as well as I, spoke of the laws of heredity as necessary arbiters of alliances, and she agreed with me that a man was justified in allowing the personality of his sweetheart's mother to weigh in the balance of his love. Such as the parent was, the daughter would be apt to be, and the irrational play of fancy should be spurred or curbed accordingly.

Taken all in all, Virginia Langford's nature was more ideally beautiful and exalted than that of any woman I had ever encountered, and I rejoiced to think that the qualities she prized in man were perhaps not lacking in me. I did not possess, to be sure, those dazzling talents which might well belong to the fortunate lover of so rare a creature; nor was I wealthy, in the sense implied by ambitious mothers when speaking of financial catches. But there was a singular unison in our ideas, a sympathy and a correlation between our thoughts in regard to the great questions of life. Her views upon the nature and development of love, for instance, seemed to me to savor of a grand unselfish selfishness, — a desire to play the part of a benefactress to the race while revelling in individual bliss. To this point the gradual development and solidifying of character had also brought me; and instead of irrational lovers, we were an earnest, deep-souled man and woman, keenly alive to the failings as well as the virtues of each other. I knew well that she had faults, and I never flattered myself that mine were concealed from her.

It is difficult to portray, so as to render interesting to others than the parties immediately

concerned, the details of our acquaintance, for,
as has already been hinted, Miss Langford was
not the kind of young woman who makes her
intimacies with the other sex conspicuous by
coquetry. She did not go out of her way to
bring about seclusion, but obliged me to seek
her society in the bosom of her family and in
the ordinary encounters of young people. She
declined to saunter by my side through retired
streets, nor did she tell me of her private affairs
more than was needful to a proper friendship.
She read the books I lent her, and asked me to
repeat many favorite passages from the same in
the dusk of the library after five-o'clock tea; but
if ever in the ecstasy of my emotions I seemed
to dwell with a personal significance on lines rich
in sentiment, the slight contraction of her brow
or deliberate coldness warned me to desist.
Shall I ever forget the stately poesy of her
figure as she descended the steps of the chapel
every Sunday morning, holding her tiny prayer-
book in her hand, her lips eloquent with a proud
but holy calm? I loved her with a devotion

that seemed to lift me above the tawdry tangle
of the world.

I do not think it was until near the end that
she was aware of her love for me. Certainly she
never realized the full force of her attachment
before the time of parting came. She was, of
course, no stranger to the fact that I loved her ;
but that might mean little to a woman at whose
shrine the lady-killers of two continents had
languished in vain, and doubtless she tried to
believe that it meant no more to her than when
others wooed. There are some, doubtless, who
will ask why it was necessary that we should
part at all. What was there to prevent the
everlasting union of two souls so completely
accordant as ours? I might, by way of reply,
point to fate as the scapegoat to which belonged
the blame of our separation, if indeed blame is
a word that can properly be employed in connection therewith. If a more explicit cause be
sought, I can only refer once more to that
allegiance to the eternal fitness of things which
we both professed. A complete and strict

abnegation of self, where the operation of the
laws of Nature was concerned, seemed to us one
of the vital virtues of society.

I had passed nearly six weeks in Baltimore
before anything occurred to suggest the likelihood of our separation in the event of her reciprocating my ardent love. One day she let
fall a remark which, like the seeds men bury in
the earth, grew silently but unfalteringly in my
mind, until its germination burst the bonds of
concealment and overshadowed my happiness.
The language I have used may sound metaphorical, but her statement was sufficiently con-
cise. There was consumption in the family.
Her mother's mother died a victim to that
fell disease, and one of her maternal uncles
was on the point of dissolution from a similar
cause.

"Ah!" I cried, "I hate to hear you say
that."

I sat back in my chair and said no more,
but I could tell from her wincing look that my
silence was more painful to her than speech.

She had tried, for both our sakes doubtless, to make the blight seem insignificant as possible; but struggle as I would, it was impossible for me to prevent the inroad of that old familiar whisper, Is this a spirit in whose companionship your every aspiration will find content?

Not so much did I yield to its influence at the time, but later, when in the seclusion of my own apartment that evening, I drew forth from its resting-place above my heart the remnant of Aunt Selina's gift, and examined it critically. All that was left of the once beautiful symbol was a segment of the size I had given dear Blanche Lombard three years before. It was months since I had looked at the trinket which now lay sadly shorn of its proportions, but still a veritable symbol of flesh and blood, in the palm of my hand. With the gentle sorrow awakened by the memory of my former loves, I recalled the old lady's trust in me, and her reliance upon my ability to avoid the family pitfall. After so many years of well-deserved encomium, was it meet that I should become recreant? Was the passion against which I had striven with so much *éclat* hitherto to usurp and conquer me now? My love of to-day had indeed a root and dignity compared to which my earlier experiences seemed merely volatile infatuation; but — ah Virginia, Virginia! an affection worthy and ennobling as ours must be self-sacrificing rather than selfish! Further delay here would be fatal, for in my weakness — who is so strong as to wrestle successfully with love? — if I were to remain I should marry her, and we, united, it is true, but none the less deliberately, should fly in the face of that grand law of the survival of the fittest, which was a light in the pathway of us both.

It is difficult to estimate precisely the relative force of the various factors that influence action. None familiar with the genuineness of my nature will doubt that I loved Virginia Langford with an intensity calculated to satisfy the ideal of those who regard the passion of a true-souled man for a woman as the champion grace. I looked upon her as the beautiful embodiment

of the quintessence of feminine qualities, and I
had never encountered her equal. Nevertheless,
I found myself handling my effects with a view
to departure, and making arrangements which,
if persevered in, would consummate a separation. I ordered my hotel bill to be prepared
for the morrow, and a berth to be engaged for
me in the sleeping-car. A force against which
I seemed to strive in vain controlled my actions.
Darling Virginia! And yet has not conscience
claims before which love's most delicious dream
must melt away, even though it dissolve in
tears?

The next afternoon I drove to the Langfords,
and, though the avowal caused me bitter tor-
ment, announced my departure on that evening.

"What! Going to-day?"

Often as I had heard those words fall from
rarely chiselled lips at similar junctures, they
never affected me so powerfully as on this occasion. Any thrill of awakened self-esteem at
the tribute to my fascinations implied in the
plaintiveness of her utterance was swallowed up

completely by the deep sense of the loss I was about to sustain.

" Yes; business of importance demands my attention. A telegram " —

I could proceed no further. My voice choked with the burden of its emotion, which I turned my head hastily away to conceal.

The drooping of her proud head upon her bosom revealed to me no secret, but the action served to confirm the resolution I had previously formed. It would be cruelty unworthy of a noble soul, not to say a gentleman, were I to defer longer the hour of parting. Even a few days of procrastination might easily render the shock of separation too rude for her endurance.

" Virginia, can you doubt for a moment I love you, and that necessity alone disunites us? "

On bended knee I seized her hand, and touched with my lips the white surface, — an unconscious action, of which I was made aware by the contact of the ·cold setting of the sapphire ring which adorned her finger. Yet, when apprized of my temerity, I pressed another chaste

kiss upon the flesh. Her hand trembled in
mine, as the earth when thunders bellow loud-
est, and, lest there might have been ambiguity
in my language, I said, —

"Truth dwells not in caves, but on the mountain tops; still, what boots a confession of love
betwixt you and me when fate, cruel as adamant
but no less unyielding, is about to tear us apart
forever."

She sought to withdraw her fingers from
my grasp, and wiped with a lace handkerchief
her lustrous eyes, where the tears had already
gathered.

"I do not understand," she murmured; and
so great was her trust in my sincerity that no
shade of the queenly *hauteur* which mantled her
air toward all others was apparent even now.

"Have you forgotten, Virginia, what you told
me yesterday?"

My phrase wore the garment of a profound
despair, but its misery paled before the anguish
which tortured her patrician profile when she
had wrung from memory the meaning of my

10

words, which did not come to her at once, but with a revelation gradual as the approach of dawn.

"Love of mine," I continued, "let us be true and steadfast to those noble principles which, if we were not the first to disclose to mankind, we can at least make permanent by example."

"Yes," she whispered; "I see, — I understand. It is impossible. You are right."

"But you love me, do you not? Oh, say that you love me! Little as I prize that virtue which is based on a system of rewards and punishments, give me, in return for this abnegation, the bliss of knowing I am not unduly confident."

For an instant she did not respond. That pride which was her noblest adornment was also her most jealous guardian. Her violet eyes, erst liquid, scintillated a strange gleam. Her frame shook, and her gentle bosom rose and fell with the spasmodic pulsation of heat-lightning. Then she turned to me, and the whole wealth of her ardent Southern nature seemed to dissipate pride, as a huge wave of the sea sweeps in a breath the deck of the stalwart ship, —

"Yes; I do love you!"

The overwhelming sweep of the ocean wave typified, too, the vehemence of my embrace, for reaching out my arms I clasped her to my breast, — her, the queenly Virginia, the superb patrician, the haughtiest and loveliest of the daughters of the South. In the impetuosity of our mutual mood our lips met in a deep, fervid kiss.

"My own, my sweet!" I murmured, "fate cannot rob us of this moment's happiness. Come what may, — and would to Heaven some dispensation of Providence may open to us the gates before which the angel of conscience stands with flaming sword, — come what may, this hour's rapture will atone for a plethora of sorrow. We must part, but I at least shall carry away with me an influence for good that will color the current of my life, and serve as a beacon and a blissful memory in outcast hours. Through your ministration, dearest, I have learned that even more noble than the capacity to appreciate a soul queenly as yours is the strength to renounce on the threshold of joy that same soul at the call of duty."

The completion of my words found her calm and composed. Her head no longer touched my shoulder, but upright and face to face we stood hand in hand. Her lips still trembled, warning me that any display of irresolution on my part would be a knife in the side of the duty to the behests of which so much deep love was to be sacrificed. A single phrase, — a mere gesture, — I ween, would have mastered her scruples and prompted her to speed with me to the altar. So deep and strong is the love of woman, that, like the pelican, she will at the last feed on that moral vigor which is as the life-blood of her being. It was I who here stood steadfast and forbade the banns.

" Is it then needful, — must we part? " she whispered.

"O darling, if conscience would but loose the seal from my lips, how gladly should I breathe accents to make you eternally radiant! Alas! there is no such boon in store for us."

We were standing in the library, surrounded by all the household gods which, associated with my darling, had become so precious to me. Her favorite books lay close at hand. A pet dog lying on the hearth-rug slept unconscious of our suffering. The tea-urn sang merrily, in evidence that Nature's laws must play the Spartan, nor falter one jot or tittle, though two hearts were breaking. Clasping her white hand once more with both of mine, I bent a passionate kiss thereon, and placed in her grasp the remnant of Aunt Selina's bauble, saying, —

"Receive this gift, insignificant though it be, in token of our friendship. Believe me, you have *all that there is of my heart!*"

I bowed, and to conceal my deep emotion left the apartment. Pausing at the bottom of the staircase, I could not forbear from looking back; perchance the rustle of her garment reached my ear. She stood erect upon the landing in all the magnificence of her statuesque misery. A look was in her eyes that went to my heart, as the arrow flies to the heart of the woodland monarch from the bow of the archer. A light gauze drapery, half fallen from her shoulders, gave to her maiden majesty the aspect of a sorrowful Diana. One moment I faltered, then speeding up the oaken stairway I was by her side. Some in my position would have fallen at her feet and said, "Let those who have no joy, hug duty;" but pressing her to my breast I kissed her with treble rapture, only to cast her loose again. In a voice hoarse with a passion that, though mastered, was still clamorous, I cried, —

"Farewell, my love, forever and forever!"

An hour later I was bowling over the railway.

Time, which had so far touched me with its finger as to cause my mother to exclaim,

as she bent over my chair on the evening of
my home return, "Why, Arthur, here is a gray
hair!" had wrought a wondrous change in the
three fair girls who rejoice to call themselves
my sisters. Alice Maud was become a slim,
dreamy-eyed maiden of eighteen summers, and
even the little Medora could no longer lay
claim to such an adjective, except by a serious
straining of the term. In one corner of the
apartment Julia Pierson was conversing with a
light-haired youth, upon whose upper lip the
fluff of a callow age had sprouted feebly.

Experience had taught me that it was useless
to strive to conceal from these beloved, but
astute, young persons the incidents of my relations with their own sex. Hence I no longer
sought to mystify them or to put them off the
scent by cunning responses. Sooner or later
they were certain to discover the real state of
the case, and taunt me exultantly. Anything
in the nature of a sentimental episode was a
source of immense excitement to each and all
of them.

"Alice Maud," said I, "you ought to go to Baltimore, if only for the pleasure of seeing the beautiful Miss Langford. She is an exquisite creature, and had I been a marrying man I should have been tempted to cast myself on my knees before her."

"Oh, why did n't you? I know I should adore her," said my eldest sister, with all the enthusiastic confidence of youth.

"But why are n't you a marrying man?" asked little Medora. "It would be lovely to have her for a sister."

"Yes, it is high time for you to be married," exclaimed my mother.

"Of course it is," broke in the head of the house, looking up from his newspaper; "I was a father at your age."

"You know that Aunt Selina says I am the Knave of Hearts," I answered quietly; and then with a sigh I added, "One cannot wed without loving."

"Certainly not," said Julia Pierson, from her corner; "but you were in love once, I am sure."

"With whom, miss, pray?"

My tone betrayed my indignation.

"Leila Johnson. I dare say she would have you if you were to ask her."

"Very likely," I responded dryly.

"She is a great deal too good for you. There!"

The eye of Julia Pierson flashed, and the youth at her side must have been surprised at such an ebullition from a child ordinarily so meek.

I laughed sardonically, and was on the point of making some cutting reply when the rustle of Aunt Selina's dress told me that my aged relative was leaving the room. As she passed my chair she let fall, it seemed to me designedly, her ball of worsted, which I proceeded to pick up. A moment's consideration decided my course of action, and I reached the threshold of her chamber shortly after she had crossed it.

"Sit down, Arthur; I must collect my breath a little," said Aunt Selina.

The poor old lady had aged much since the day she last had done me the honors of her apartment. The crow's-feet had furrowed deeper lines in her withered countenance, and her peaked chin was almost a point. Her ferret eyes, however, still glittered keenly as of yore, and though she hobbled painfully, there was elasticity in her demeanor.

Despite her remark, she did not at once sit down, but proceeded to rummage in her ancient mahogany escritoire, whence she took out the package of letters tied about with a faded lavender ribbon, which I had seen at our previous interview. She likewise produced from the closet another bottle of the old Madeira I had enjoyed so greatly.

"This is the last bottle, my dear. There is no such wine in the country."

"You are quite right, aunt. Its peer does not exist."

She watched me sip the golden fluid.

"Arthur," she said, "I am glad to see you again. You are a great comfort to me."

I bowed gravely, and raised my glass again, with a gesture implying that I drank her health.

"Your sisters," she observed, "have disappointed me."

"Scarcely that, I should say, aunt. There was little reason to believe that their evolution would be satisfactory."

"You are right, dear. I always prophesied that they would develop the family failing."

"Ripe apples are not more certain to fall to earth at the breath of Boreas than my sisters to repair to the altar at an early age," I responded laconically.

"Julia Pierson is the worst," said the old lady. "She has a sentimental interest already in the fair-haired stripling below; but it is not concerning them, but you, that I desire to speak. I am an old woman, and my days hardly will outlast the fragrant wine you are quaffing."

She paused, moved by the reflection, and I endeavored to put into pleasing speech the hope and conviction that she would live to see many a vintage gathered.

"No, no, flatterer!" she cried. "I am only a withered leaf which the first breeze will loosen from the bough."

Still she seemed pleased at my observation, and helped herself to Madeira before proceeding.

"Arthur, I wish to intrust to your keeping all that I possess of value, so that in the event of my death no unsympathetic eyes may peep at my secret. This miniature" (here she fumbled in her pocket and reproduced the familiar leather case) "you already know. These letters are the archives of a love which, though sepulchred, still lives in all its old-time vigor. But yet this packet contains one piece of parchment, the perusal of which will not fail to cause you surprise, and it may be pity, for the poor relative whose executor you are about to become. Receive them, my nephew, but without comment, pray. When I am dust, you will find no difficulty in solving this enigma."

I took the packet and miniature from her trembling hand, though not before she had opened the case and pressed a burning kiss upon the features of the dashing youth there reproduced. Tears streamed from her aged eyes, and while she sought to stem their force by means of her yellow lace handkerchief I turned my head discreetly away. When I renewed my gaze in her direction I was surprised to find that she was smiling at me through her tears. In a cracked, fiendish treble that had more of the witch in its cadence than any sound to which I had ever listened, the aged spinster uttered these words as she raised her glass to her lips : —

"I drink to the Knave of Hearts. Ha! ha!"

"Madam," said I, with dignified decorum, though shuddering a little withal, "your most obedient."

It is my custom when partaking of a beverage to look over the rim of the glass rather than into it. As I swallowed the rare liquor with a deliberation due to its quality I became aware that Aunt Selina's features were undergoing a change. She gasped once or twice, and half rose from her chair in the exquisiteness of her

efforts. I sprang from mine to assist her, but
before I could reach her side the shrivelled
dame fell back inert and wax-like. Aunt Selina
was dead!

V.

WHEN I alighted from the Bar Harbor steamer, three months later, I was wearing a weed on my hat of the width appropriate to one mourning a great-great-aunt. The Professor, who again came to meet me, glanced at this badge of sorrow critically but respectfully, as I answered, in response to a remark of his concerning sundry festivities, that I expected to be very quiet.

"Oh, I had n't heard," he said.

"Yes, I have lost my great-great-aunt on my father's side."

The Professor was silent a minute. Presently he inquired, —

"Did she leave you anything?"

"Nothing to speak of," was my reply.

"Oh!"

The Professor asked no more questions, but evidently did not regard my affliction as inconsistent with his whistling softly the air known as "Over the Garden Wall."

"May Corcoran is down here."

"Is she?" I responded, with quiet indifference.

"Yes, and so is Maud Bittinger. I told them both you were coming."

Miss Bittinger was a young lady who stood number four on the list of those with whom I had been intimate.

"Professor," I said calmly, "I have come to Bar Harbor for meditation, not to seek society. I have reason to believe that the woman does not exist who can bring the flush of interest to my cheek."

"Dear heart!" said the Professor, "is it as bad as that?" He did not speak for some moments. At last he said, "There is one girl down here whom I wish you would tackle.

Any number of men have come to grief in that direction."

I laughed the half-scornful, half-amused laugh of one used to easy conquest, —

"Have you tried your hand on her, Professor?"

"Yes," he whispered. "You need n't publish it, but I have. Between you and me, I worked hard for nearly a fortnight. It was no use, though; she did n't weaken in the least."

He seesawed his hand while talking, by way of emphasis.

"Her name is Mabel Westering," he continued.

"Westering?"

"Yes; do you know her? I believe she comes from Chicago."

"No; I have never heard of her before."

I was a little interested, however, by the coincidence of the name. Could she by any possibility belong to the family of Aunt Selina's sweetheart, I wondered, with a sort of lazy speculation.

We were walking up the road from the pier, and so familiar was I with the surroundings that I failed even to scan the beautiful faces visible at almost every step. I felt that I had already ample acquaintance with the various types of womanhood, and I experienced somewhat the sensations of one who beholds in the morning light the scene of last evening's banquet.

" She is tall and stately," said the Professor, " with dark chestnut hair and deep brown eyes. She has read everything, and she's the best climber in the place. She takes long walks by herself. The story is," he added somewhat ruefully, " she says there isn't a man here worth bothering her head about. There's your chance, Arthur."

" Have n't I told you already that I'm not in the mood for anything of the kind? Besides, when a man gets to our age, Professor, he has run across about every pattern of fair one there is. I 've gone through the list pretty thoroughly."

" I know," he answered, shaking his head; " but she is something unique."

"*Nous verrons,*" I said, with quiet confidence,
and hummed the words of the Shakespearean
verse, —

> " Why, let the strucken deer go weep,
>   The hart ungalled play ;
> For some must watch, while some must sleep ;
>   So runs the world away."

That day I spent in the privacy of my apartments, putting my things to rights. Toward
evenfall, indeed, I sauntered out for a short
time to breathe the fresh, invigorating air. I
felt contemplative, and far from inclined for adventure. To tell the truth, from a strange dread
of what might be the character of Aunt Selina's
secret, I had delayed examining the packet in-
trusted to my keeping. She had been in the
tomb three months, but the reluctance of my
constant nature to anticipate change and alter
the peacefulness of the present had made me
dilatory in the consummation of this last
funeral rite.

My own private reflections were also of a
morbid order. The intense yearning to en-

counter some spirit in whose companionship
my every aspiration would find content was still
rife within me, and as my eyes traced the thin
glittering streak of the new moon down the
evening sky, my bosom thrilled with exquisite
emotion. And yet the next instant the remembrance overcame me that I was as distant from
the goal as ever, and the soul was still to be
found whose affinity for mine was such as the
earth for the rain-cloud. But should I ever
meet a spirit of so rare a texture? Were not
my aspirations so completely refined and ethe-
realized as to preclude my encountering a kindred nature in the realms of matter? I had no
wish to be supersubtle in detecting blemishes in
the sweet maidens whose hearts were exposed to
my attractions; but had not my powers of criti-
cism and discernment become so far magnified
by experience as to be able to perceive flaws that
escaped the observation of minds more superficial? The dreadful fear lest I had reached a
state which lifted me above the category of
human lovers stalked at my side like a spectre.

Such thoughts for many weeks had preyed upon my mind, and they were still a part of my consciousness, when, staff in hand, I started upon the following day to seek a spot safe from scrutiny, where I might sit and investigate Aunt Selina's packet. I walked for several miles through fern and brake, and then branched off and pursued a direct line toward the shore. An intimate knowledge of the coast revealed to me shortly the access to a smooth ledge, which the ebb tide leaves uncovered just in the jaw of a precipitous chasm. It requires some skill as a rambler to be willing to select so retired a resting-place, for the spot in question lies several hundred feet below the bank, and is only to be reached by a sheer and difficult descent. Nevertheless, when once the obstacles are overcome the lover of Nature's beauties is amply rewarded. I found myself on the brink of a foaming flood, which surged in eddying currents of creamy white and lucent green around the base of the bowlder on which I was sitting, and, twisting away into the bowels of the chasm

beyond, laved its towering walls with columns
of spray. The broad expanse of the deep
stretched away to the horizon, and the curves
of the shore brought into relief on either hand
jagged spurs of crag-beetling cliffs, and rocks
fringed with the brown mane of ocean.

"Aunt Selina, dear Aunt Selina!" So I
prefaced my examination of the packet tied
with the faded lavender ribbon. There were no
human ears to hear my soliloquy; only the sea-
gulls, that with strident cries circled above my
head.

The letters were seemingly those of an ardent, generous nature. Their phrases savored
little of the cautious conservatism of the present day. They suggested rather the free, un-
fettered play of the sea, which he who penned
them gloried in. Some were mere scraps, written at odd moments, when love's lightning entered the sailor's soul and bade him strike.
Others were redolent with the fragrant perfume
of poesy, exhumed at quiet hours, in the exu-
berance of leisure. So, at least, I judged the

garnered correspondence of the pirate captain,
whose trophy was the heart of my maiden aunt.
Long as the lapse of years must have seemed
to her true spirit, his death could not rob her of
these sweet memories. In their old-fashioned
way, this couple had doubtless realized much of
the intensity of love. Why should it not have
been so? They were too undeveloped to understand the long-drawn-out rapture of a soul susceptible and yearning as mine. Time — that
great unsealer of secrets — granted, it is true, to
Aunt Selina to discern the possibility of a more
complete happiness than she had known; but
such is the fate of all who outlive the methods of their own generation. It is essential to
human progress that we should rise to higher
things on the stepping-stones of our dead
selves. Age sees the error of its spring-tide
days, and loves to play the pilot and mentor
to adolescence.

As thus I pondered, I was holding between
my fingers a letter written in a different hand
from the others, and addressed —

To

MISTRESS SELINA LATTIMER, SpInster,

Att ye Port of Boston,

Massachusetts Bay.

Unfolding the document, the seal of which other hands than mine had sundered, I read as follows : —

LONDON.

WORSHIPFUL MISTRESS : It having pleased the Almighty God to order it that myselfe & my two bigest sons tho small should be left fatherless by ye death of Captain Michael Westering late mariner of his Majesty his service, — my youngest son having been lost in ye barque Phantom with his father, my husbãd — I have found among ye papers of ye late departed sundry memorials of his early days, namely : One miniature, one packet of letters signed "yr. loving and soon to be partaker of your joys and sorrows, Selina," one needle-boke in ye shape of a heart marked with ye leters S. L. to M. W., and fashioned doubtles for service on ye deep where women folk be not mostly.   Being in great difficultyes, sore pressed to raise moneys and knowing yt my husband died having ye fear of God in mind, with repentãce for hys former sins, I make bolde to ofer these relicks to your consideration, yett for hard cashe nevertheless, — to wit £10 lawful money

of ye realm — So be it yt you have desire to hold
comunication with me regarding ye same relicks or
memorials adress Mistress Alice Westering at ye sign
of ye Blue Lion, Fleet Street, and am

Your very Ready and obediĕt servant.

A. W.

P. S. — One Paul Jones, a publisher, who purposes
to make a record of doings of my deceased husbād
in hys book of famous pirates is willyng to give me
£6 for the writyngs.

My feelings during the perusal of this ex-
traordinary composition were of an acute order.
It was thus apparent that my late lamented aunt
had lived for many years the possessor of a secret which must have gnawed at her very heart-
strings. Whilst all the world believed her lover
to be sleeping at the bottom of the sea, near to
the coast of Guinea, the faithless pirate had
broken faith with the maiden who had bestowed
upon him her pure, devoted heart, and wedded
another, — another, who ten years later had not
been too delicate nor too proud to practise
petty blackmail on her unfortunate rival.

Poor Aunt Selina! This, then, was the mystery which had served to jaundice the aged spinster's disposition, and caused her to regard a complete surrender of the affections in early youth as a badge of folly. The explanation of her desire to save me from a fate similar to hers — to withhold me from a bestowal of my whole heart until discretion came with the increase of years — was now manifest. She had discerned in me a yearning susceptibility which, unless judicious counsel was at hand, would speedily plunge me into hopeless difficulty. She had seen that, if left to my own devices, the veriest chit of a maid might have played fast and loose with my love. And so she had spoken; so she had taken me aside and said: "My son, let us reason together." It was her admonitions that had been a light to my feet through the mazy fields of festivity, where infatuation lurks behind each hedgerow and fancy plays the will-o'-the-wisp to the understanding. Instinctively I took from my pocket the note-book which contained the chronicle of my experiences since the day Aunt Selina first favored me with her counsel, and ran my eye over its pages. Only a few hours before I had conceived the idea of making a summary or condensation of its contents, just as a banker balances his books at the close of the year, and I had drawn up a statement to the following effect: —

August 1, 1881.

Blanche Lombard,		To
May Corcoran,		Arthur
Cora A. Delaney,	Spinsters.	Lattimer,
Maud Bittinger,		Esq.,
Henrietta Milford Davis,		Bachelor,
Virginia Langford,		*Drs.*

To one heart.

ITEMIZED ACCOUNT.

———— $\frac{1}{6}$

1.

January, 1878.

Blanche Lombard, of New York, N. Y.

Blonde; superb physique; fine animal spirits; giggles.

" You horrid thing ; I never will speak to you again."

2.   ——— $\frac{1}{6}$

August, 1878.

MAY CORCORAN, of Philadelphia, Penn.

Brunette; rare intelligence; speaking eyes; wears the look of a woman in search of a happiness of which she has dreamed but never experienced.

"I have known all my life what it is to struggle against fate. I am quite alone in the world. I am an orphan."

3.   ——— $\frac{1}{6}$

February, 1879.

CORA E. DELANEY, of Chicago, Ill.

Petite, bewitching; vivacious; very small hands and feet; black snappy eyes.

Prefers to be called "Miss Birdie" by her "gentlemen friends."

"Ma always leaves the room when I have company."

4.   ——— $\frac{1}{6}$

July, 1879.

MAUD BITTINGER, of Albany, N. Y.

Tall, graceful, dignified; lineal descendant of a Patroon; slight foreign accent; loves books; dresses well.

"Have you read Dante, Mr. Lattimer?"

"I wish you would tell me my faults.   There is

nothing I think more undignified than confidences between persons who are almost strangers ; but where there is perfect friendship and reliance on both sides I believe in throwing off reserve."

5.

July, 1880.

$\dfrac{1}{6}$

HENRIETTA MILFORD DAVIS, of Germantown, Penn.

Quaker origin ; simple, quiet, reserved ; a pure, child-like nature.

"I do not care for excitement. Give me a peaceful country nook and one congenial friend and I am happy."

6.

March, 1881.

$\dfrac{1}{6}$

VIRGINIA LANGFORD, of Baltimore, Md.

Elegant, accomplished, statuesque ; black hair ; a light coloring ; violet eyes.

"But he would always have the counsel of England's maiden queen as a mentor, 'If thy heart fails thee, climb not at all.'"

Total, one whole heart.

Respectfully submitted,

ARTHUR LATTIMER, *Knave of Hearts.*

E. and O. E.

The reading of this account in its entirety, following as it did the discovery of Aunt Selina's secret, served to throw a still deeper shadow athwart the current of my thoughts. For the first time I realized my own actual condition. It came over me as I sat on the brink of the foaming surge that I had given away my whole heart by piecemeal, and was a bankrupt, so to speak, at the court of love. Now I understood that the morbid and despondent feelings which had haunted me of late were but the undefined consciousness of this state. Aunt Selina and I had been alike victimized by causes the anti- podes of each other. We had given our hearts away and received nothing in return, though hers had been bestowed in one sweet breath, and mine doled out by inches.

  "*Incides in Scyllam cupiens vitare Charybdim;*"

or, as Shakespeare has it, "Thus, when I shun Scylla, your father, I fall into Charybdis, your mother." The classical allusion was indeed germane to my condition, for had I not, in the effort to avoid the pitfall so fatal to my great-aunt's happiness, compromised my own by straying too far upon the other side? My heart was gone. With all my capacity for loving, I had lost the power to love. My relative's passion had been lavished in the bulk, while I had apportioned mine in driblets. Yet it had been reserved for us both to awake and find an insolvent world our debtor.

The hoarse swash of the waves, now grown louder, harmonized with my miserable mood. I could have thrown myself into them, and hushed forever the dreadful whirl of existence, for aught I cared to live, with the power to love no longer rife within me. Like the silence which follows when the last chord of the harp snaps beneath the touch of the silver-haired minstrel was the solitude of my soul. I drew from my pocket the lancet given me by Aunt Selina, which bore as the termination of its handle a minikin of a Cupid, and tossed it from me into the boiling waters. What did the glittering token avail me, now that the heart which

yielded to its keen touch was consumed? Even
as Arthur, Excalibur, so cast I the silver guerdon
into the dark water; and as it flashed upon the
surface I almost fancied that, as in the old-time
legend, a white hand caught and shook thrice,
ere it vanished from sight, the precious emblem.
It was an old woman's hand, and no wedding-
ring encircled the third wasted finger.

I do not know precisely how long I sat
thereafter gazing at the creamy eddies and over
the billowy expanse of sea, so lost was I in the
isolation of my thoughts. I was brought back
to actuality by a crashing sound close behind
me. Looking over my shoulder, I beheld the
remains of a lady's parasol, which plainly had
been let fall from the brow of the cliff. It had
struck the ledge a few feet in my rear, and the
force of the shock had shattered the point.
The handle, however, was still intact, and as I
seized it in order to snatch the implement from
the greedy usurpation of the breakers, I observed with curiosity that my fingers encountered a minikin of a Cupid precisely similar to

the device which adorned my ci-devant lancet.
Raising my eyes, I discerned a tall and graceful
girl upon the edge of the bluff above. Even at
the great distance which separated us I thought
I could perceive a blush upon her cheek as
though she were aghast at her clumsiness, or
rather her apparent artifice to attract my attention, which to a sensitive soul would be a source
of galling discomfiture, for none but the veriest
novice would stoop to such an inartistic method
of making an acquaintance.

But not for an instant did I impute to her so
ungenerous a suspicion, for I could plainly see
that she was a young lady whose experience of
life had been ample and far from superficial.
There was nothing of the tyro in her garb or
figure, as she stood out in relief against the afternoon sky. With a bold and practised step I
began to scale the heights which towered betwixt us, with her sun-umbrella in my teeth.
Athlete as I was, I could not keep my eyes
fixed upon her person, except transiently, for
the ascent was one of difficulty.

At last I conquered the opposing distance
and stood erect upon the bluff, which was richly
carpeted with greensward. My glance fell upon
a girl of rare and perfect beauty, the character
of whose garments was rendered of minor importance by the consummate grace with which
she wore them. I simply took note of a large
hat girdling her face like a halo. It was
trimmed with a waving feather, black and
glossy as a raven's plume, and only second
to her lustrous hair. But the features were
what riveted and enthralled my attention.
Where before had I beheld the eyes radiant
with keen vitality which looked out at me from
under those dark tresses? From what niche
in memory's hall had those dashing, proud
lineaments descended to mock me with their
presence? I could not tell, and under the ban
of my perplexity I stood staring in her face
a longer time than was consistent with complete decorum. Doubtless she interpreted my
bewilderment as effrontery, and concluded that
I suspected her of design in the catastrophe to

her parasol, for her air became haughty; and though she thanked me as she received the broken complement to her costume from my hand, her manner implied that she did not intend the incident to be made use of as the opening wedge to an acquaintance.

The downheartedness of my mood reacting from the elasticity which had prompted me to play the gallant, supplied me straightway with an antidote to her suspicion.

" Madam," said I, — and I made use of this appellative to clothe my speech with as much dignity as was possible, — " in happier moments I should perchance have ventured to express the desire for an introduction to one whom I have had the honor and good fortune to succor; but private grief of a character too intricate for a passing utterance has robbed me of the spirit of enterprise by which I was formerly possessed."

I saw in an instant that my words aroused her interest. They were, as I intended, ornate, and removed from the usual form of address.

It had been palpable to me that nothing short of a marked individuality would engage her attention, and I was able to feel now that her wide experience did not include a man of my properties. Her features relaxed in haughtiness, and her eyes betrayed a glimmer of coquetry as she replied, somewhat after my own fashion, —

" However that may be, sir, you have not forgotten the art of chivalry. I grieve that my unseemly interruption should have broken the thread of reflections, which, though melancholy, ought to have been sacred."

I answered, this time with a slight tinge of reserve, that she need feel no concern upon that score, for mine was a grief which flourished in any soil, nor could be affected by circumstances. In regard to her estimate of my gallantry, I added that I trusted no one would ever find me deficient where the welfare or comfort of one of her sex was involved.

She plucked mechanically one of those tall succulent strands which grow where grass is

abundant, and twirled it pensively. I was
manifestly an enigma to her, and doubtless
doubly so from the fact that she was wont to
find most men very easy to understand. I
cannot say it was material to me, feeling the
burden of my sorrow so keenly, whether or
not she saw fit to prolong the interview. Still
I stood pondering on her beauty, and wondering where I had seen her features before.

She looked up at me suddenly and said,
evidently in pursuance of a deliberate resolution, —

"Are you, then, among those who find the
silent sympathy of Nature's forces more consolatory than the language of friendship?"

She looked modest and self-contained, but
wore that expression of exquisite interest which
I had often noted upon the countenances of the
flirtatious. I recognized that I was face to face
with an adept, and one who would be quick to
detect anything which was commonplace or
inartistic in my social sword-play. I was equal
to the occasion.

"Madam," said I again, with an increased frigidity, "I have already implied that were I in the condition of one whose emotions were unhampered, I should be quick to acknowledge and pay tribute to the fascinations concentered in a beautiful woman; but such is not the case. Your words are but the ordinary prelude to a coquettish intimacy, — the bait which, under the guise of psychological abstraction, conceals the hook of personal ambition. Waste not your time on me, I pray, for without prejudice to your powers of attraction I should prove an unprofitable subject. You have, I will assume, encountered in your day many curious types of the creature man; but, methinks, you for the first time are in the presence of one whose heart has been eaten away piece by piece, even as the rock is eaten by the sea, until no vestige of it remains. The love you would fain awaken in my breast abides there no more. I am impervious to the fascination of woman."

As I spoke I perceived the blood mantle her cheeks, until they glowed a very crimson. Her eyes flashed with spirited resentment. Yet she did not interrupt me; and as I finished, the color of her complexion subsided and a clever smile curved her lips. She gazed at me with a renewed interest before she replied, —

"We are, then, comrades in misfortune."

"Madam," said I slowly, "I recognize no such tie. Believe me, I am in earnest when I tell you that I have outlived the capacity of reciprocating affection. No wile, however skilful, can decoy me from my isolation."

She tapped her boot softly with the rescued parasol.

"You do not, I think, understand me."

I shook my head sadly, but with decision.

"It is without prejudice to your charms, I repeat, when I say that, though you were to dally with me for a twelvemonth, I should still be marble."

"Sir," she resumed more haughtily, "I have given you credit for much discernment of a certain kind. You showed yourself a keen observer of the ways of woman in alluding to a former phrase of mine as a bait to conceal the hook of personal ambition. Your words were not devoid of talent. But lost in the selfishness of one consideration, you have failed to grasp a truth analogous to your own, and quite as genuine. Your genius has its limitations."

Even now I hesitated, fearing lest her language veiled a cunning ruse to ensnare me into a flirtation. Nevertheless I observed that I had no wish to forfeit any esteem she might have seen fit to honor me with.

"Why should we not," I added, "since I have defined my position clearly, seat ourselves on the grass, for it is still far from twilight."

She accepted this semblance of an apology, and composed herself upon the greensward. However, she was silent, and made little holes in the loam with a pointed pebble. I examined her more closely. Somewhere, surely, I had beheld those striking features.

Suddenly she turned to me and said with a quiet smile, —

"You have given me to understand that the

nature of woman has become so far cloying to you as to fail to impress you even when most ideally represented in the flesh."

"Yes," I replied; "I can say, without exaggeration or boastfulness, that I am thoroughly intimate with the feminine disposition. The woman does not live, I think, whose character I should not be able to fathom in a few minutes' interview."

"You speak with confidence."

"Yes, madam; and as your tone implies a doubt as to my ability to prove the secret springs which dictate your conduct, I shall be bold enough to class you in the school of those who seek to impress men by the apparent intensity of their sympathies, — a school, indeed, most attractive and formidable, but innocuous to me, who am beyond the influence of any woman."

She laughed a low, scornful laugh, and then sighed deeply.

"There was a time when a boast such as yours would have weighed less heavily upon my pride than the foam of the billows upon the

bosom of the ocean. Even six months ago I
should, despite your assurance, have found it
no difficult task, I ween, to inscribe your name
among those who have owed me fealty."

I shrugged my shoulders with quiet amuse-
ment.

"But," she continued, "the time for that has
passed. Grant, if you wish, that I was such a
one as you describe, an adept at bringing your
sex to their knees by force of my sympathetic
demeanor, I am no longer free to practise such
amenities. Or, to phrase it more justly, as it
seems to me, I once could love with a passionate
fervor, but, like you, my heart is now dry as the
fountain parched by the summer's heat. Here,"
she added, "if you doubt me, is the proof."

She put her hand into her pocket and drew
forth a note-book which she passed to me for
inspection. Then covering her face she wept
silently. I could see the drops forcing a passage betwixt her fingers. With grave curiosity
I undid the clasp, and to my vast amazement
read as follows: —

August 1, 1881.   BAR HARBOR, Maine.

CHARLES LEROY,
DONALD K. TIMMINS,
HARRY FOSDICK,   To
MILTON PARKER,   } Bachelors. {   MABEL
E. OPDYKE MANCHESTER,   WESTERING,
JACK KING,   Spinster,
                                  Drs.

To one heart.

ITEMIZED ACCOUNT.

1.   ——— $\frac{1}{6}$

January, 1878.

CHARLES LEROY, of New York, N. Y.

Handsome, muscular, an Adonis of a man; very silent; rowed in his class crew.

"Oh, Miss Westerly, I'm not clever, I know, but I *do* love you so."

2.   ——— $\frac{1}{6}$

July, 1878.

DONALD K. TIMMINS, of Baltimore, Md.

Lithe, graceful, and agile; a fine tennis player; padtlles beautifully; sings divinely; rather a nice brown mustache.

"My life has not amounted to much; but if you — Mabel — would consent to share my poverty, I should work very, very hard."

——— $\frac{1}{6}$

3.

February, 1879.

HARRY FOSDICK, of Philadelphia, Penn.

Stylish, dashing; black, wavy mustache; dresses beautifully (papa says he's rather fast); sends lovely flowers.

"I will not pretend to deny that I have paid devotion to other women in the course of my life; but you will believe me, dearest, I feel sure, when I say you are the only woman I have ever loved."

——— $\frac{1}{6}$

4.

July, 1879.

MILTON PARKER, of Boston, Mass.

Refined, dignified; has nice respectful manners; carefully trimmed side-whiskers.

"It is now three months, Miss Westering, since I spoke to you before on this subject. I have been faithful to the words I then uttered, that I could not forget you. I love you with all my heart. Only this time I feel I owe to myself and my prospect in life to say, 'Take me or leave me.'"

Turning over the page, I saw that the episodes which followed were to the same general
effect. It was plain that her experience had
been literally a parallel of my own. Her love,
like mine, had been drawn upon until the sacred
font of passion had become exhausted. My
eyes were moist with tears as I gazed at my
neighbor, who still sat with shrouded face.

"Miss Westering,—Mabel," said I, "we are
indeed companions in misery. It is only just
that you should read my experiences, also."

I handed her my note-book.

I watched her open my memorials. At the
sight of my name she gave a little exclamation,
and looked at me scrutinizingly for an instant.
The contents interested her, plainly, but seemed
to increase her despondency, doubtless from
the analogy of the various incidents to her own
experiences.

Meanwhile I, with a stealthy gesture, drew
forth the miniature of Aunt Selina's lover, and
opening the leather case gazed upon the features
there portrayed. A single glance told me that

my conjecture was correct, and that the similarity of the names was no mere incident of chance. The dashing mien, sparkling eyes, and raven's-wing locks of Captain Westering were reproduced in the beauteous maid at my elbow. It seemed verily as if fate had brought us together to typify the truth of the prophecy that the sins of the fathers are visited upon the children. The guiltless as well as the guilty are called to suffer in this unequal world. Through the deceit practised by her ancestor upon mine, a pair of innocent lives had been brought face to face with unhappiness.

She finished the inspection of the note-book and looked up at me with a sad smile.

"It is strange, is it not?" she said.

"Yes, Mabel Westering, and even stranger still to one who holds the key to the mystery."

She blushed as though fearful of my meaning, and gazed at me with vivid eagerness.

"What! are you — is it possible you are related to the Miss Selina Lattimer whose miniature is in my possession?"

She fumbled in her pocket.

I bowed my head.

"She was my great-great-aunt. And you, Miss Westering, I take to be a lineal descendant of that faithless man who robbed my ancestress of her maiden love. Behold his likeness."

Each simultaneously reached to the other a leather case of the same proportions, and in silence, though her cheeks were aflame, we studied the features of our respective relatives.

Mabel was the first to speak: "He was my great-grandfather."

"And a pirate," I added bitterly.

Her eyes flashed defiance.

"You are cruel," she murmured.

Even then I realized that her reproach was not without justice. What had she done, poor child, to deserve my censure? My mood should rather be stirred to compassion by the mutuality of our misfortune than egged to vengeance by memories of ancestral wrongs. Yet I could not for a moment school my feelings to a due

clemency, so guileless and trusting were the
maiden features of my injured kinswoman, looking at me from the ancient portrait.   At last I
said, with gentle melancholy, —

"It is not meet that I should blame you,
Mabel.   We are alike unhappy from causes
brought into being ere we were born.   If it will
not add to your sorrow, I would fain show you,
however, a letter written by your great-grandmother.   It was she who was the occasion that
Captain Westering proved faithless to his troth,
and in the perusal of this document you will
perchance find an excuse for my hasty words."

She inclined her head gratefully and received
the aged parchment, which she read with
attention.

" My great-grandmother wronged your Aunt
Selina bitterly, Arthur," she said.   " I am very
sorry."

" This, I presume, is the miniature there
referred to ? "

" I believe so, Arthur."

I was silent a moment.

"How has it chanced, Mabel, that you have come to such a pass as you describe? Was there any incentive in your case that prompted you to be chary of bestowing your heart? I was a victim to an ancestral desire for vengeance; but you, — how has it happened that you are no longer susceptible to that exquisite passion which sways the world?"

"I know not, Arthur, to what to ascribe it, save my blood."

"True," I murmured; "it was in your blood. You are a prey to the vampire heredity, poor girl!"

"I can only say that I am very wretched, Arthur."

I had not intended to express more than the interest of genuine pity, and no vestige — at least designedly — of a more ardent emotion filled my breast. But the guise of Mabel Westering's last expression and the look imprinted on her face put me on my guard. The frequent use of my Christian name, always couched more tenderly than my utterance of hers, likewise attracted my attention, and I could not help experiencing the impression that, despite her assertion to the contrary, Mabel Westering's heart was still susceptible to a fascination such as I had the power to exert. Brought face to face with this conclusion, I will admit that the desire for revenge for an instant was superior to more worthy sentiments, and I almost embraced the opportunity offered to play the part of a deceiver for the sake of Aunt Selina. But those lofty principles of action which had hitherto been my counsellors came to the rescue once again, and saved me from an act which, however pardonable under the circumstances, would still have been malicious. These reflections sped with arrow-like rapidity through my mind, and I said, —

"Miss Westering, indeed we are both very wretched. In the language of the dramatist, I may well remark, 'A plague on both our houses.'"

I was silent for a little, and pulled my mustache pensively.

"I would it were possible," I continued, "for us to emulate the example of that old-time pair of lovers who, despite the rancor of family hatred, plighted their troths because sweet love willed it so." I thought I discerned a slight tremor on her lips, and the color in her cheeks came and went as I spoke. "But, alas! neither for you nor for me is so happy a termination to our misery possible. There is a premise lacking which cannot be supplied. Love is wanting, and without it Romeo's ladder no longer appeals to the imagination. Regard it neither as flattery nor yet discourtesy if I say, that though I discern in your charms that which might easily have brought me to your feet in days now past forever, I am at this moment an indifferent beholder of those same fascinations."

I paused; and I must do her the justice to say that, however much she may have been drawn toward me, pride now came to her rescue and clothed her language with appropriate dignity.

"You are intelligible, Mr. Lattimer, and I

appreciate that you do not desire to wound me. Permit me in turn to state that, though you were to proffer me on bended knee a heart new found, I should not know where to seek for love wherewith to reciprocate your bounty."

" I shall, at least," I added, trusting thereby to smooth the way to parting, " carry away with me the remembrance that another exists, no less unhappy than myself, to whom I can turn in the hour of need for sympathy."

She had quite regained her ancient *aplomb* and serenity.

" See," she observed, pointing to the western sky, " yon molten cloud awakes more sympathy in me than all the race of man."

I bowed with consummate grace, and so we parted.

A week later I was at home once more, and several people spoke of the middle-aged appearance that seemed to have settled upon me. My barber said my hair was getting very thin on top.

I found my dear sisters in the neutral tints which separate mourning attire from gay apparel. They were enjoying the pleasures of the summer season after the manner of young ladies of social position and culture. I met Alice Maud strolling along a byway, on the day after my arrival, with a young man upon whose lip the question so fateful to feminine welfare faltered, — but merely from bashfulness.

It was on the third day that Julia Pierson took me apart and whispered — I must do her the justice to say she had developed into a stylish-looking girl — whispered that she was engaged.

"What!" I cried, "to that" — I was going to add "callow, tow-headed youth," but I forbore.

"Yes, Arthur, Mr. Plympton."

I kissed my second sister with genuine affection.

"I am *so* happy, Arthur. I do wish you would follow my example."

I stroked the golden hair of the earnest supplicant, and a tear-drop bedewed my eye.

"I'm sure Leila Johnson would forgive you, if you were to ask her," added Julia Pierson.

I sighed, and though my hand ceased to caress the smooth tresses, it still rested fondly thereon.

"Well, well, child! who knows what the end may be?"

www.ingramcontent.com/pod-product-compliance
Lightning Source LLC
Chambersburg PA
CBHW030835270326
41928CB00007B/1062